S.D. Roberts

UNIX
XENIX & VENIX

**Introduction
Applications
Tips & Tricks**

PREFACE

The UNIX operating system is becoming one of the
favorite and most commonly used operating systems.

The fact that 16-bit computers are becoming the
standard for microcomputers, and the falling prices
for fixed disks, make UNIX an interesting operating
system even for the low end of the business
microcomputers.

The purpose of this book is to introduce the layman
to the UNIX operating system environment.

The large number of examples in this book makes it
easy to follow and understand.

For the development of this book, we had an ALTOS
586 with the XENIX operating system, which is
similar to the UNIX operating system.

We wish all readers of this book a good time
programming in UNIX.

TABLE OF CONTENTS

Some notes about this book.

This book was written for the UNIX beginner. It is a
self-study course.

The reader of this book creates his own surroundings
in UNIX. The samples used are based upon each other.

Only the most often-used commands are described.
These commands may be slightly different between the
different versions of UNIX.

This book is suited perfectly as an introduction for
the layman, i.e. for someone who has never heard
anything about UNIX except the name.

It is a good idea to go through the book quickly
before you turn on your computer with the UNIX
operating system. This will give you a rough idea
about what is going on. Afterwards, you should turn
on your computer and try all the examples. This
should be fun since it will give you a sense of
achievement.

Once you have gone through the book and typed in all
the examples you should be able to use the UNIX
operating system to do most jobs required.

UNIX   1

1.1 Introduction

UNIX is one of the most successful operating systems today, although it is more than ten years old. UNIX was developed at Bell Laboratories in New Jersey.

UNIX is available today for all major computers. The precondition for running UNIX is a minimum of 256k of RAM and a fixed disk with a minimum of 10Mbyte.

1.2 How UNIX emerged

In the years 1965 through 1969, an operating system was developed in a combined project of Bell Laboratories, General Electric (Honeywell), and MIT. The operating system was to be named MULTICS.

MULTICS was a very complex system which required a big computer like the GE 645. MULTICS was a multi-user timesharing system which could serve a large number of users at the same time.

In 1969 Bell Laboratories retired from the MULTICS project. Several employees of Bell secretly decided to develop a smaller and more compact operating system. These employees, under the leadership of Ken Thompson, wanted to develop a system for their own research and development. The first operational UNIX system was written completely in machine language on a DEC PDP-7.

In the meantime, the programming language B by Ken Thompson was developed into the high level language C by Dennis Ritchie at Bell Laboratories. This C language today is linked to UNIX in most cases.

UNIX was now rewritten in C. The advantage of this was that the operating system became more transportable. Just 5 to 10% of UNIX remained in machine language. A disadvantage of this was that UNIX became a lot bigger.

UNIX also became available for the PDP-11, which is a very popular computer with universities and colleges.

In 1973, Western Electric agreed to distribute UNIX in license to universities and non-commercial companies.

By 1975 UNIX had become very popular in universities, and Bell came out with the first commercial version of UNIX. This version was called Version 6; it is still in use today.

In 1979 Version 7, a completely redone product, came out on the market.

1.3 The most common versions of UNIX

UNIX originally was written with the PDP-11 in mind. Later it was implemented on other computers as well. Examples are the IBM PC, the ALTOS, the SAGE II, etc.

1.3.1 UNIX-V7

This UNIX version has major improvements over its predecessors. Files can be up to one billion bytes long, and the portability of the system has been improved. The C language was improved. The shell interpreter was equipped with string handling and error tracking. Structured programming became possible. UNIX-V7 shows the efforts by Bell to make UNIX more commercial.

1.3.2 UNIX SYSTEM III and SYSTEM V

UNIX SYSTEM III was developed from UNIX-V7 by AT&T. This version is the most important one at the moment because it even works on small computers such as the ALTOS, for example.

There are no big differences from UNIX-V7. The SCCS (Source Code Control System) was taken over from the UNIX-PWB (Programmers Work Bench). The system is designed for connection to large computers and networks.

The latest version introduced by AT&T is SYSTEM V. AT&T claims that all future versions of UNIX will be compatible with SYSTEM V.

1.3.3 UNIX-BSD 4.2 (Berkeley UNIX)

Aside from AT&T, UNIX was improved upon and developed at the University of Berkley.

Many UNIX users claim this to be the best UNIX version. The Berkley UNIX uses virtual memory, a more user-friendly C shell interpreter, and a full screen editor (VI). Beside that, some other commands have been added. UNIX-BSD 4.2 is relatively small so that it can fit on smaller computers.

1.3.4 XENIX

XENIX is an operating system similar to UNIX. It was developed by Microsoft, which is known for MS-DOS and MBASIC. XENIX is like SYSTEM III, a development of UNIX-V7. For that reason it is very similar to SYSTEM III.
XENIX is available for IBM PC, TRS 16, LISA (APPLE), ALTOS 586, COMPAQ PLUS, etc. XENIX is a so-called UNIX-like operating system.

IDRIS is a so-called UNIX lookalike operating system. That means IDRIS creates the impression of being a UNIX operating system.

The operator doesn't recognize that he is working with a different operating system. IDRIS works on the SAGE II. More about IDRIS and SAGE in a later chapter.

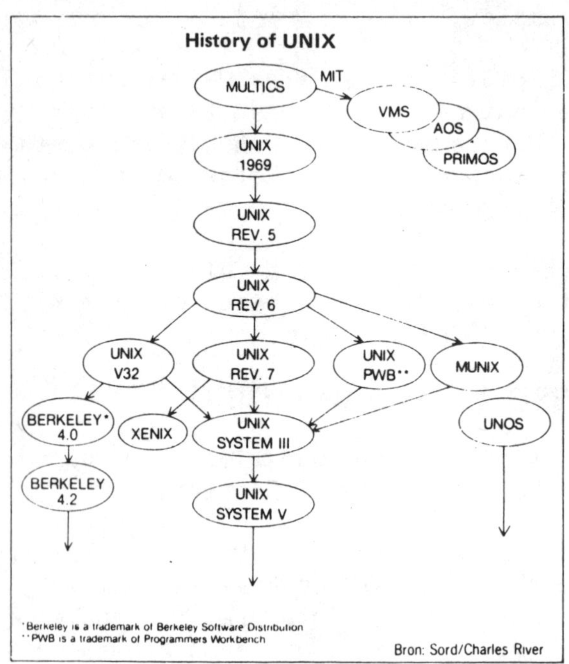

1.4 Disadvantages of UNIX

Besides the advantages of UNIX (portability, flexibility, modularity, user friendliness, low license fees), there are also some disadvantages.

One of the biggest disadvantages is that there are so many different versions of UNIX. There is definitely a lack of a standard.

Another disadvantage is the size of the operating system. The size actually limits this operating system to fast 16-bit computers. There has to be at least 256k of RAM and a fixed disk. 8-bit computers are thus excluded. Only the newer microprocessors such as the 68000, 68020 by Motorola, the 80286 by Intel, or the Zilog 8000 are suitable.

Another big disadvantage of UNIX is that it is not suited for realtime applications. UNIX is a multiuser, timesharing system where several users work on the computer at the same time. The switching from one process to the next one, called dispatch function, is relatively slow in UNIX. There are UNIX-like operating systems that don't have that disadvantage, such as UNOS.

1.5 Applications for UNIX

Since a lot of software already exists for UNIX, the applications are numerous. UNIX can be found in managament, development, and executive offices.

1.5.1 UNIX in the office

The UNIX operating system itself contains a lot of user software. A good wordprocessor (NROFF), for example, is included.

There are, of course, excellent wordprocessors for UNIX available from several software manufacturers.

Software for appointment scheduling (calendering) and electronic mail is included also. There is even software available for typesetting.

1.5.2 UNIX in the development department

It comes as no surprise that UNIX can be used in development, because that is the environment UNIX was originally developed for.

Besides large mathematical programs, there are software packages available for CAD (Computer Aided Design).

There are also several cross-assemblers available so that it is possible to develop programs for different computers.

1.5.3 UNIX in management

For the manager there are more and more productivity tools available that work under UNIX.

There are several decision helper programs available. These programs generate a graphical display of data from a data base. It is possible to check the effects of changes on the whole situation (future projection).

1.6 What languages, data bases, and networking utilities are available for UNIX?

Normally a UNIX system contains a lot of user software, for example the following languages are usually included:

    -C (the system language)
    -FORTRAN 77 (structured FORTRAN)
    -SNOBOL
    -RATFOR (mixture of C and FORTRAN)
    -EFL
    -BAS (some kind of Tiny-BASIC)

Besides that the following is available through software manufacturers:

    -COBOL
    -BASIC
    -FORTRAN IV
    -PASCAL
    -ADA (soon)

In terms of DBMS (Data Base Management System), the
following is available:

    -DB-SYS
    -INGERS (Berkeley)
    -LOGIX
    -MARATHON
    -MISTRESS
    -ORACLE
    -PHACT
    -POLARIS (Bell)
    -UNIFY
    -YARD

It is possible to link several UNIX systems through
networks. As far as we are informed, the following
systems can be used with UNIX:

    -XEROX-Ethernet
    -Corvus-Omninet
    -ZILOG Z-Net
    -ALTOS-Net
    -BBNET by AT&T

The software for UNIX systems listed above is just a
small part of what is available.

1.7 Important terms

Some important terms used in conjunction with UNIX
should be described here.

Multiuser System

A multiuser system is a system which allows several
users to work on the computer at the same time. Most
of the time each user has his own identification and
password, so that only an authorized person gets
access to the system.

Timesharing System

In a timesharing system the processor is assigned only temporarily to a certain user, but each user gets the impression that the computer is working full time for him or her. A timesharing system is usually a multiuser system.
The disadvantage of a timesharing system is that if many users occupy the computer at the same time, the speed of execution slows down considerably.

Cross Compiler and Cross Assembler

These are utilities which allow one to develop a program for computer B on computer A. The developed program is assembled or compiled by the cross assembler/cross compiler and will run on computer B, not on computer A.
These utilities allow you, for example, to develop an operating system for one computer on another computer.
Example:
A program developed on a COMPAQ PLUS with 68000 cross assembler will run on a Macintosh, but will not run on a COMPAQ.

DBMS (Data Base Management System)

DBMS programs allow you to manage data stored in a data base. It allows you to add new data, search for data, delete data, and edit data. A DBMS program is the interface between the user and the data base.

First contact with UNIX 2

This chapter is meant for the UNIX layman who comes into contact with UNIX the very first time.

2.1 LOGIN

First of all you have to go to your system operator to get your user i.d. and your password. Once you have gotten these two words you can go to your terminal and turn it on. The following should appear on your screen:

    login:

This is the prompt telling you to enter your user i.d. If something else or nothing at all appears on your screen, contact the system operator. Usually the problem is found relatively quickly.
If the prompt appeared on the screen, enter your i.d., for example:

    login: elcomp

UNIX will answer with:

    Password:

At this point enter the password you got from the system operator.
Don't be surprised if nothing is displayed on the screen when you enter your password. The echo of your password is not displayed on purpose because nobody should be able to read the word on the screen.

If you make a mistake typing in your password, the
following will be displayed:

    login: elcomp
    Password:
    login incorrect
    login:

You are asked to enter your i.d. and your password
again. If you can't get into the system at all,
contact your system operator.

If everything is entered correctly, a message
similar to the one below should be displayed:

    XENIX Version 2.5a

    $

On your terminal you might get something different
from "XENIX Version 2.5a". This message tells you
which system you are using. In our case it was a
XENIX operating system installed on an ALTOS 586
computer.

The dollar sign is the so-called prompt. This
character tells us that UNIX (or XENIX in our case)
is ready to accept commands.

Sometimes the date or messages from the system
operator are displayed also.

Succeeding chapters deal with the different commands
available   and techniques to define   your   own
commands.

To get something on your screen, enter the following
now:

    $ date

Note:
You don't have to enter the Dollar-sign of course.
If "date" was entered correctly, something like this
should be displayed:

    Wed Jul 18 08:20:26 1984

You will get a different date and time, of course.
Command "date" displays the day of the week, the
month, the day, the exact time, and the year. After
the date is displayed, UNIX waits for the next
command. This is indicated again by the Dollar-sign.

NOTES

Files and the editor 3

In this chapter we will talk about files with UNIX and how files can be created using the editor "ed" which is included in the UNIX operating system. Each sample is accompanied by a listing showing what happens on the screen.

3.1 What is a file?

A file is a certain group of characters belonging together. This group of characters has a name, the file name.

The characters can be a program, text, or certain other data.

How do you determine which type of file you have ? The UNIX command to determine this is:

```
$ ls
```

After you have entered this command, you should get a list of different files, normally the files in your directory. If you have just started though, there is nothing in your directory, so you will get the following display:

```
$ ls
$
```

This comes as no surprise to us because we haven't created a file yet.

The next chapter tells how to create a file using the editor.

3.2 The editor "ed"

After "date" and "ls" we introduce the third command here, the call to the editor.

If you call the editor, you should enter a file name as a parameter along with the editor command. This file name can be the name of an already existing file (if you want to edit an existing text), or a new name.

Enter the following command:

    $ ed sample

This is a call to the editor with the parameter "sample", which is the name of the file to be created. The editor will answer with:

    ?sample

The cursor is at the beginning of the next line. Now you can enter commands. The message "?sample" means that the editor does not know a file called "sample". This is understandable because we are just now creating the file.

Before we enter text, a few words about the keyboard are in order.

Every keyboard is a little bit different, but certain keys are on every one. Every keyboard has a control key (Ctrl). This key always is pressed in conjunction with another key. The key for deleting a character is called RUBOUT, or DEL, or BACKSPACE. With UNIX you can use this key to delete the character entered last. If you want to delete the whole line, enter Ctrl-U, that means while you are holding down the Ctrl-key, press the U-key.

The first file we are going to create is a text
file. Before we enter the actual file, we have to
enter 'a' for 'append' as follows:

```
?sample
a
```

Now the text can be entered line by line. Each line
is terminated by the Return-key. Enter the text now
as shown below.

```
?sample
a
This text is used to show the different commands of the
UNIX standard editor.
The editor is called with "ed", usually followed by a file name.
Although this editor is a so-called line oriented editor
it is very powerful because of its many commands.
We will talk about the majority of these commands in this chapter.
You might ask yourself why it is so important to know the
editor first of all.
The answer to this is, that the editor allows you to write data,
or programs, or texts to the floppy disk or to the fixed disk.
.
```

The period at the end of the text terminates the
input. Please note that this period has to be the
only character in a separate line. Now we want to
save our text on disk. This is done with command
"w".

```
?sample
a
This text is used to show the different commands of the
UNIX standard editor.
The editor is called with "ed", usually followed by a file name.
Although this editor is a so-called line oriented editor
it is very powerful because of its many commands.
We will talk about the majority of these commands in this chapter.
You might ask yourself why it is so important to know the
editor first of all.
The answer to this is, that the editor allows you to write data,
or programs, or texts to the floppy disk or to the fixed disk.
.
w
524
q
$
```

After you enter the "w" a number will be displayed.
This number indicates how many characters the file
is long. Command "q" stands for quit. With this
command you leave the editor. The dollar sign shows

us that we are back at the command level. Let's
enter the ls-command now:

```
   $ ls
   sample
   $
```

As you can see, this command shows us the name of
the only file in our directory.

Another command shows us the contents of a file.
This command is command "cat". Enter the following:

```
   $ cat sample
```

This lists the contents of the file sample on the
screen:

```
$ cat sample
This text is used to show the different commands of the
UNIX standard editor.
The editor is called with "ed", usually followed by a file name.
Although this editor is a so-called line oriented editor
it is very powerful because of its many commands.
We will talk about the majority of these commands in this chapter.
You might ask yourself why it is so important to know the
editor first of all.
The answer to this is, that the editor allows you to write data,
or programs, or texts to the floppy disk or to the fixed disk.
$
```

3.3 The editor commands

We are going to check the commands available from
the editor using our sample. Because of the great
number of commands available in the editor, we can
only talk about the most important commands here.

We load the editor and our sample file with the
following command:

```
   $ ed sample
   524
```

This time we don't get a question mark because the
file "sample" already exists. Instead the size of
the file (number of characters) is displayed.

3.3.1 Line numbers and general structure of the command

Every line entered gets a corresponding number. This number indicates which line, counting from the beginning of the file, it represents. The first line is number one. Since the number of the last line of the text normally is not known, because it constantly changes, this line gets a special character: the dollar-sign.

As mentioned before, the line numbers are for addressing the single lines. Almost all commands need a line number or a range of line numbers. All commands have the following structure:

    (start,end) command

The parentheses indicate that the actual address sometimes is optional. "start" as well as "end" are arithmetical expressions. Not all commands need an "end" expression.

3.3.2 Moving around the lines

If we want to look at a particular line, we enter this lines number. For example if we want to see the third line, we enter a "3" followed by Return.

3
The editor is called with "ed", usually followed by a file name.

The third line gets displayed. If we press Return now, the fourth line will be displayed.

3
The editor is called with "ed", usually followed by a file name.

Although this editor is a so-called line oriented editor

Repeated pressing of the Return key brings us to
the end of the text.

```
editor first of all.

The answer to this is, that the editor allows you to write data,

or programs, or texts to the floppy disk or to the fixed disk.

?
```

The question mark indicates that the end of the text
has been reached. If we want to go backwards, we
enter a minus-sign ("-").

```
-
The answer to this is, that the editor allows you to write data,
```

Entering a plus-sign has the same effect as pressing
the Return key.
A minus-sign/plus-sign followed by a number moves
backward/forward that number of lines.

```
-3
We will talk about the majority of these commands in this chapter.
+3
The answer to this is, that the editor allows you to write data,
```

In the above example we first moved back three lines
and then forward three lines, so that we are back
where we started.

Using plus and minus signs, we can generate
arithmetical expressions.

```
-3+4-1+5-3-2
The answer to this is, that the editor allows you to write data,
-3+4-5+3
editor first of all.
```

The first expression caused nothing at all, because
the result of the arithmetical expression is zero.
The second expression causes a jump backward by one
line.

The character for the current line is the period
with the editor. If you want to know which value the
period currently has (actual line number), enter the
equate sign ("=") after the period.

```
.=
9
```

In the example above the current line is line 9.

3.3.3 The print command

If we want to see the current line, we enter:

```
p
editor first of all.
```

We could have entered ".p" as well. Instead of the period, we can also enter an arithmetical expression. For example, if we want to see the first line we enter:

```
1p
This text is used to show the different commands of the
```

Note:
The above command also changes the current line number to 1.

Instead of defining one line, we can also define a whole range of lines:

```
1,3p
This text is used to show the different commands of the
UNIX standard editor.
The editor is called with "ed", usually followed by a file name.
```

The above command displays the first three lines of our text. The expression "1,3" results in command "p" affecting lines 1,2, and 3.

Command "1,$p" displays the whole text, first line through last line. Command ".,$p" displays all lines from the current line through the last line.

Instead of numbers or special characters, we can use mathematical expressions, too.

```
$-2,$p
editor first of all.
The answer to this is, that the editor allows you to write data,
or programs, or texts to the floppy disk or to the fixed disk.
```

The above command displays the last three lines of the file (if the current line was the last line).

3.3.4 Inserting, deleting, changing of lines

3.3.4.1 The append command

We already know this command. We used this command to enter our sample text file. This command appends text entered to the current line. This is shown in the example below:

```
a
These two lines were added behind the current line, which is
also the last line, using the append command.
.
```

The period terminates the input as usual.

If we enter a number or an arithmetical expression in front of the "a", we can use this command to insert text anywhere in the file. This is shown in the example below:

```
2a
This text contains typos.
```

The new line has been inserted behind the second line. It became the new line 3.
We can take a look at the changes to our text:

```
1,$p
This text is used to show the different commands of the
UNIX standard editor.
This text contains typos.
The editor is called with "ed", usually followed by a file name.
Although this editor is a so-called line oriented editor
it is very powerful because of its many commands.
We will talk about the majority of these commands in this chapter.
You might ask yourself why it is so important to know the
editor first of all.
The answer to this is, that the editor allows you to write data,
or programs, or texts to the floppy disk or to the fixed disk.
These two lines were added behind the current line, which is
also the last line, using the append command.
```

3.3.4.2 Inserting lines

Instead of inserting new lines behind existing ones
we can also insert in front of a certain line. In
this example we want to insert in front of the first
line. This would be the same as an append after line
zero (0a).

```
1i
The UNIX-editor "ed".
```

We have inserted two lines now (the second line is
empty). This can be checked with the following
command:

```
1,4p
The UNIX editor "ed"

This text is used to show the different commands of the
UNIX standard editor.
```

3.3.4.3 Deletion of text lines

With the editor you can not only insert, but you
also can delete lines of text. A lower case "d" is
used for the delete command. It is possible to
delete a single line or a range of lines. A plain
"d" deletes the current line.

```
d
```

deletes the fourth line in our example. To check
that we enter "1,4p".

```
1,4p
The UNIX editor "ed"

This text is used to show the different commands of the
This text contains typos.
```

As you can see the line actually got deleted.
The next example shows how a range of lines can be
deleted at once.

```
$-1,$d
```

This command deleted the last two lines of our text.
We can verify that now.


```
1,$p
The UNIX editor "ed"

This text is used to show the different commands of the
This text contains typos.
The editor is called with "ed", usually followed by a file name.
Although this editor is a so-called line oriented editor
it is very powerful because of its many commands.
We will talk about the majority of these commands in this chapter.
You might ask yourself why it is so important to know the
editor first of all.
The answer to this is, that the editor allows you to write data,
or programs, or texts to the floppy disk or to the fixed disk.
```


As you can see, the command created the result
wished.

Warning!
Command "1,$d" deletes the whole text !

3.3.4:4 Changing lines

The editor has a command which is a combination of
insert and delete. This command allows you to change
lines. This command, written as "c", first deletes
the specified line and then inserts the new text
entered for this line. The following example changes
the third line of the text.

```
3c
This line was changed using the "c"-command.
.
```

The period, again, is the terminator.
Command "3c" did the same as "3d" followed by "2a"
would have done. It is possible to use this command
for several lines as well. This is shown in the
following example:

```
9,10c
Why learn the editor first?
```

The altered text now appears as follows:

```
1,$p
The UNIX editor "ed"

This line was changed with the change command.
This text contains typos.
The editor is called with "ed", usually followed by a file name.
Although this editor is a so-called line oriented editor
it is very powerful because of its many commands.
We will talk about the majority of these commands in this chapter.
Why learn the editor first?
The answer to this is, that the editor allows you to write data,
or programs, or texts to the floppy disk or to the fixed disk.
```

As you can see lines 9 and 10 have been deleted and
the new line has been inserted after line 8.

3.3.5 Search and replacement of text

3.3.5.1 Search for text

Sometimes you want to search for a certain "string"
in your text. A "string" can be a single character,
a word, or several words.
The editor allows you to do that easily.
Let's say we want to search for the next occurrence
of the word "editor" in our text. To do that we
enter:

```
/editor/
The UNIX editor "ed"
```

As you can see the editor found the first line. When
we printed our text (that was the preceding
command), the last line of the text became the
current line. The search command works in a so-
called wraparound way; that means when it reaches
the end of the text, it continues the search at the
beginning of the text.

If we now want to search for the next occurrence of
the word "editor", we just have to enter the
following:

// /
The editor is called with "ed", usually followed by a file name.

The editor stored the string we are searching for.

The search starts at the current line and works towards the end of the text. If you want to search backwards, the slashes ("/") have to be replaced by question marks ("?").

    ?editor?
    The UNIX editor "ed"

As you can see, the editor has found the preceding line, which is the first line. We could have gotten the same result with "??".

3.3.5.2 Substitution of text

It sometimes happens that just one word in a line has to be changed or added. In this case, it would be impractical if the whole line had to be entered again. For this case, the editor has the command "s" for substitute. If no line number is specified this command works on the current line. It is possible to enter a range of lines with this command. The following example changes "ed" to "ED" in the current line:

    s/"ed"/"ED"/

Between the first and the second slash is the string to be replaced. Between the second and the third slash is the replacement string. In other words, the first string is replaced by the second.

We can look at the changed line using command "p".

    p
    The UNIX editor "ED"

The two commands (substitute and print) can be combined:

```
s/"ED"/"ed"/p
The UNIX-editor "ed"
```

This command changes the line back to its original condition and lists it.

The next example shows how text can be replaced throughout a certain range of the text.
If we want to change the word "file" into "FILE" throughout the whole text, we can do that with the following command:

```
1,$s/file/FILE/p
The editor is called with "ed", usually followed by a FILE name.
```

The "p" entered additionally does not print all lines that were changed, only the line changed last. This line also becomes the current line.

Next we want to change all letters "o" to "?". This is done by the following command:

```
1,$s/o/?/p
?r programs, or texts to the floppy disk or to the fixed disk.
```

As you can see, only the first "o" has been changed in the last line. The same is the case for all the other lines of the text, because the substitute command only replaces the first occurrence of the specified string in each line. If we want to change that, we have to add a "g" (for global) to the command.

```
1,$s/o/?/gp
?r pr?grams, ?r texts t? the fl?ppy disk ?r t? the fixed disk.
```

The p at the end lists the line changed last. The changes were made throughout the whole text. We can check that by listing the whole text:

```
1,$p
The UNIX edit?r "ed"

This line was changed with the change c?mmand.
This text c?ntains typ?s.
The edit?r is called with "ed", usually f?ll?wed by a FILE name.
Alth?ugh this edit?r is a s?-called line ?riented edit?r
it is very p?werful because ?f its many c?mmands.
We will talk ab?ut the maj?rity ?f these c?mmands in this chapter.
Why learn the edit?r first?
The answer t? this is, that the edit?r all?ws y?u t? write data,
?r pr?grams, ?r texts t? the fl?ppy disk ?r t? the fixed disk.
```

3.3.6 Another way of addressing lines

Besides entering the corresponding number, lines can
be addressed another way. This addressing uses a
certain string to be matched. A new command, command
"g" (for global) is used here. The "g" is followed
by a string between slashes:

```
g/is/p
This line was changed with the change c?mmand.
This text c?ntains typ?s.
The edit?r is called with "ed", usually f?ll?wed by a FILE name.
Alth?ugh this edit?r is a s?-called line ?riented edit?r
it is very p?werful because ?f its many c?mmands.
We will talk ab?ut the maj?rity ?f these c?mmands in this chapter.
The answer t? this is, that the edit?r all?ws y?u t? write data,
?r pr?grams, ?r texts t? the fl?ppy disk ?r t? the fixed disk.
```

As you can see, all lines containing the string "is"
are printed. Command "p" at the end is not even
neccessary, the lines are printed automatically.

If we want to change the question marks back into
"o" in all lines containing the string "is", we can
enter the following:

```
g/is/s/?/o/gp
This line was changed with the change command.
This text contains typos.
The editor is called with "ed", usually followed by a FILE name.
Although this editor is a so-called line oriented editor
it is very powerful because of its many commands.
We will talk about the majority of these commands in this chapter.
The answer to this is, that the editor allows you to write data,
or programs, or texts to the floppy disk or to the fixed disk.
```

As you can see all lines that have been changed are printed. The reason for this is that the global-command executes the whole set of commands after the second slash for each line.

The opposite of the global-command is command "v" which selects the lines that do not contain a specified string. Example:

```
v/is/
```

This line was changed with the change command.
The answer to this is, that the editor allows you to write data,

All lines that do not contain the string "is" are printed.

Note:
The string "is," is not recognized as string "is"!
Only the string "is" is a correct target. The "is" in "This" is not recognized!

Line addressing through strings is not only possible with the global-command, the following command is also totally legal:

```
1,/This/p
The UNIX edit?r "ed"
```

This line was changed with the change command.
As you can see all lines up to the line with the first occurrence of the string "This" are printed.

The command "/This/,/is/p" prints all lines from the first occurrence of string "This" to the first occurrence of the string "is".

3.3.7 Characters with special meanings

The characters ^,$,.,[],*,& have special meanings with string searching. Since these characters tend to confuse the beginner, we will not talk about them in detail. We will just mention their meanings and ways to use these characters so that they are interpreted as normal text rather than control characters.

```
^  stands for beginning of line
$  stands for end of line
.  stands for any character
[] between these characters are optional
   characters
*  any times current character
&  string just found
\  next character to be interpreted as normal
   character
```

If you want to search for one of these characters in your text, you have to precede them with a backslash (\). For example the following two commands have totally different meanings:

```
g/hello$/   and   g/hello\$/
```

The first command searches for all lines ending with "hello". The second command searches for all lines containing the string "hello$".

In the second command, the real dollar-sign is searched for. In the first command, the dollar-sign stands for the end of the line.

3.3.8 Very useful commands

3.3.8.1 Copying of text

The editor allows you to copy lines from one part of the text to another part. The command for this is "t" for "transfer".

```
3,4t$
```

This command copies the third and the fourth line to the end of the text.

```
1,$p
The UNIX edit?r "ed"

This line was changed with the change command.
This text contains typos.
The editor is called with "ed", usually followed by a FILE name.
Although this editor is a so-called line oriented editor
it is very powerful because of its many commands.
We will talk about the majority of these commands in this chapter.
Why learn the edit?r first?
The answer to this is, that the editor allows you to write data,
or programs, or texts to the floppy disk or to the fixed disk.
This line was changed with the change command.
This text contains typos.
```

The copy command is structured as follows:

```
from,to t destination
```

3.3.8.2 Moving of text

The difference between copying text and moving text
is that with moving, the original text is deleted,
while with copying it is not.
The following example shows how the third and fourth
lines are moved behind the fifth line.

```
3,4m5
```

If we take a look at the text now we can see that
the third and fourth lines became the fourth and
fifth lines.

```
1,$p
The UNIX edit?r "ed"

The editor is called with "ed", usually followed by a FILE name.
This line was changed with the change command.
This text contains typos.
Although this editor is a so-called line oriented editor
it is very powerful because of its many commands.
We will talk about the majority of these commands in this chapter.
Why learn the edit?r first?
The answer to this is, that the editor allows you to write data,
or programs, or texts to the floppy disk or to the fixed disk.
This line was changed with the change command.
This text contains typos.
```

The move command is structured as follows:

```
from,to m destination
```

3.3.8.3 Insertion of other text files

It is possible to insert another text file into the current text file. The command that accomplishes this is command "r" for "read". If we want to insert our text at the end of the text in memory, we would enter:

```
$r sample
524
```

The whole text (524 characters) is inserted behind the existing text ($). The effect is the same as if the file had been appended to the existing file. The structure of the command is as follows:

```
destination r filename
```

The file is inserted behind the specified line (destination). If no line is specified, the last line is assumed.

3.3.8.4 Display of control characters

Most texts contain some control characters, like Tabs, for example. These characters are inserted in the text by pressing the Ctrl-key in combination with another key. Most of these characters are invisible, but sometimes you want to see these characters in your text. This is accomplished by using command "L" instead of command "p" when listing the text.

Note:
<Ctrl-I> means you have to hold down the Ctrl-key and then press the I-key at the same time.

```
a
<CTRL-I> this is a Tab
<CTRL-G> this is a bell
<CTRL-A> this is a CTRL-A
```

```
$-2,$p
        this is a Tab
 this is a bell
 this is a CTRL-A

?
$-2,$l
>this is a Tab
\07 this is a bell
\01 this is a CTRL-A
```

As you can see, when using command "p" the control
characters are not displayed, while with command "L"
symbols are displayed. With command "p" the Tab
(Ctrl-I) was shown as a Tab (indented text) and
command Ctrl-G could be noted as a beep. With
command "L" a ">" is shown for the Tab and the rest
of the control characters are shown as a backslash
followed by the ASCII value of the control character
(ASCII is an international code used for
characters).

The "L" command is well suited for error tracing. It
sometimes happens that control characters are
entered inadvertently, and these control characters
can cause problems. For example, if you enter the
source code of a program with the editor, and you
then try to translate this source code later.

Let's delete the control characters now because they
might disturb us with later samples with the editor.
The following command does that for us:

    $-2,$d

3.3.8.5 Saving the text

If we are finished entering our text, we use command
"w" (for write) to save the text on the disk. This
command saves the text under the name we entered
when we called the editor (in our case, the name
"sample").

If we want to save the text under a different name, we can do that with a "w" followed by a name. For example, if we want to save our text under the name "text2" we enter:

    w text2
    1087

This command saves the text we have changed under a new name. The old text remains unchanged in the file "sample".

It is possible to use the "w" command to save just parts of the text. In this case we have to specify which line numbers we want to save.

    1,5w part1
    160

This command saves the first five lines under the name "part1".

3.3.8.6 Execution of Shell commands

The editor allows the user to execute a so-called Shell command during editing of a file. We already know some of these commands, which we called the UNIX commands. One example is the "ls" command. This command displays a list of the files we have in our directory. In order to execute such a command from the editor, it has to be preceeded by an exclamation mark. Example:

    !ls
    sample part1 text2
    !

The second exclamation mark is from the editor. It shows us that we are back in the editor. What the Shell actually is will be described in a later chapter.

3.3.8.7 Leaving the editor

If we are finished editing our text we can leave the
editor using command "q" for "quit".
If the text has been changed but not saved yet with
the "w" command, the editor will display a question
mark. This reminds us that the text has been changed
but not saved yet. If we enter "q" again, we will
leave the editor nevertheless. The changed text will
not be saved. If the text was saved, a single "q" is
enough to leave the editor.

```
q
$
```

The dollar-sign shows us that we are back in the
Shell.

3.3.9 Error messages of the editor

There is only one error message in the editor, and
this is the question mark. What error caused the
error message has to be found out by the user. This
is a disadvantage of the editor, but it conforms
with the philosophy of UNIX.

NOTES

4

The UNIX File System

We now know what a file is. What we didn't know until now is that UNIX has three types of files. These are normal files, directories, and so-called special files.

The files we used in the preceding chapter are of the first type: the normal files. The environment of these files is of the second type.

The terminal with keyboard and monitor is a file of the third type, a special file.

4.1 Normal Files

Normal files are actually all text files and the commands we enter. That's about all we have to say about normal files in this context.

4.2 Directories

To explain the term directory, we first have to explain the file structure of UNIX.
The UNIX file structure is a so-called tree. A tree, as everybody knows, has a root, a trunk, and branches with leaves. The UNIX file structure is similar. UNIX has a root, the single files are the leaves, and the directories are the branches. The figure below shows us a UNIX tree.

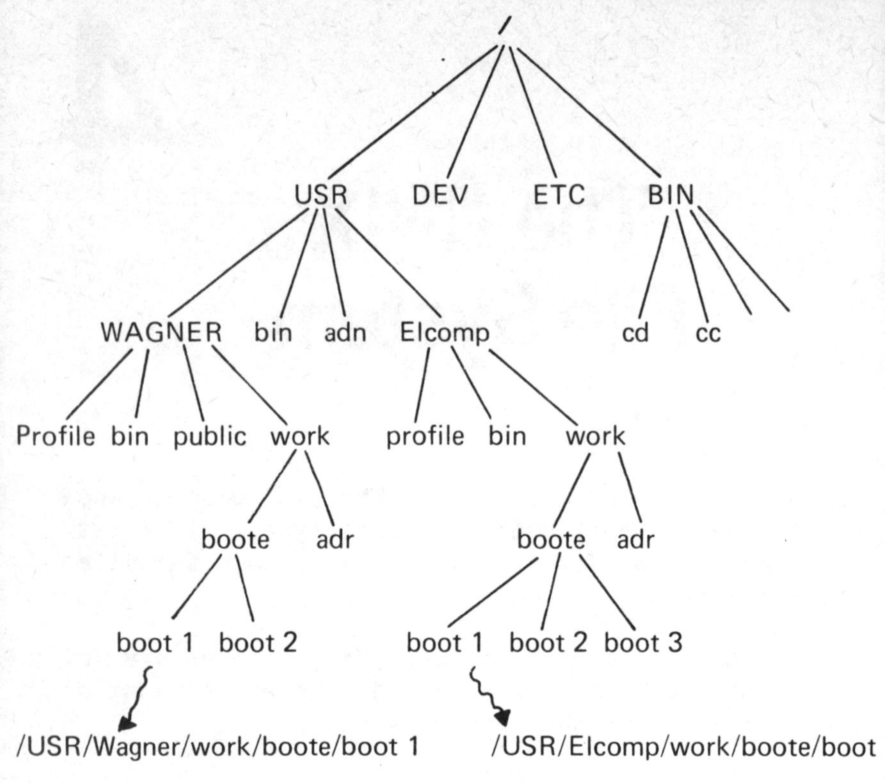

A part of our UNIX tree

The root and the trunk of the tree form the root of
our directory. It also is called "root" in UNIX. You
might call the root the mother (or father) of all
files.   The   root   has   several   branches   and the
branches can have other branches and leaves. It is
important that there is only one way to each leave
and branch in the tree.

Command   "pwd"   shows   us   the   directory   we   are
currently in:

```
$ pwd
/usr/elcomp
```

The output shows us that we are in the directory called "elcomp". It also shows us the path from the root to this directory. The root is marked by a slash ("/").

The output tells us that we have to go from the root to the directory "usr" and from there to the directory "elcomp". The second slash does not point at the root; it is the delimiter between father and son. In our system of directories, there is only one directory with this path. It is possible to have another directory called "elcomp", but in this case there has to be a different path to the other "elcomp" directory. You might compare this to two sons both named "Jim", where one Jim is your son, and the other one is your neighbor's son. Both have the name Jim, but their path to the root is different.

4.2.1 Going through the UNIX tree

We can switch between the different directories of the tree. The command for this is "cd" for "change directory". The command usually is followed by a name of a directory. For example, if we enter the following:

```
$ cd sample
sample: bad directory
$
```

We obviously made a mistake here. We used the name of a file instead of the name of a directory.

If we enter the following:

```
$ cd /
$
```

we get to the root of our system. We can check this with "ls":

```
$ ls
.profile        bin             dev             etc             f0
f1              lib             tmp             usr             venix
```

We are now in the root directory. From here we can
go to different directories. Let's go to the
directory "usr":

```
    $ cd usr
    $
```

If we enter "ls" now, we get the directories and
files stored under this directory name.

```
$ ls
adm             bin             demo            dict      dos
elcomp          games           guest           help      include
lib             spool           vgraph_demo
$
```

In your system this listing might look different,
but on any system there is a directory called "usr".
The following directory also is on most systems:

```
    $ cd games
    $
```

This directory contains the standard collection of
games in UNIX. On some systems, this directory is
not accessible at all times, the system operator
usually excludes this directory during work hours so
that people are not seduced.

If we enter "ls" now, we get a listing of games
available on our system.

The path to the directory we are currently in can be
printed. The command for this is "pwd" (print
working directory).

```
    $ pwd
    /usr/games
    $
```

How do we get back to the original directory now?
The answer is: through a plain "cd".

```
    $ cd
    $
```

You may check that with the "pwd" command.
We could have used the path "/usr/games" to get into
the games directory with one step.

```
$ cd /usr/games
$ pwd
/usr/games
$
```

Now we enter "cd" again.

```
$ cd
$
```


4.2.2 How to create a directory

Each user gets his own directory in a UNIX system.
This so-called home directory is the directory you
are in when you log in. If you want to create your
own file system, you will have to create your own
directories. The command to create a directory is
"mkdir" followed by the name of the directory to be
created.

```
$ mkdir texts
$
```

Some readers may know this command from MS—DOS.
Enter "ls" now to see what happened:

(listing goes here)

As you can see a new file "texts" is in the list.
This is not a normal file, it is a new directory.
With command "cd texts" we get to the new directory.

```
$ cd texts
$
```


If we enter "ls" we see that this directory is
empty.
Command "pwd" delivers the following:

```
$ pwd
/usr/elcomp/texts
$
```

The path became longer by one directory now. Command
"cd .." brings us back to the father directory of
"texts".

```
$ cd ..
$
```

The two periods refer to the father directory. A
plain "cd" would have done the same, of course.

4.3 Copying of files

Command "cp" (copy) allows us to make a copy of a
file. The following example shows this command:

```
$ cp sample copy
$
```

The file "copy" now is a copy of the file "sample".
You can check that with command "cat":

```
$ cat copy
This text is used to show the different commands of the
UNIX standard editor.
The editor is called with "ed", usually followed by a file name.
Although this editor is a so-called line oriented editor
it is very powerful because of its many commands.
We will talk about the majority of these commands in this chapter.
You might ask yourself why it is so important to know the
editor first of all.
The answer to this is, that the editor allows you to write data,
or programs, or texts to the floppy disk or to the fixed disk.
$
```

We can also see the new file if we enter "ls":

```
$ ls
sample  copy  part1  text2
$
```

Next we want to copy our files into the newly
created directory "texts".
To do this we have to enter the name of the file to
be copied and the name of the resulting file. The
name of the resulting file has the following
structure:

    texts/oldname

That means the copy commands have the following
structure:

    cp oldname texts/oldname

The effect of this structure is that the files in
the new directory will have the same names as the
original files. We enter the following commands:

    $ cp sample texts/sample
    $ cp part1 texts/part1
    $ cp text2 texts/text2
    $

Now we use the "cd" command to get to the directory
"texts" where we enter "ls" to look at the contents
of the directory.

    $ cd texts
    $ ls
    sample   part1   text2
    $

As you can see the directory is not empty anymore.
It contains the files we created earlier in our home
directory. This example shows that a pathname can be
used as the destination for the copy command. A
plain file name would refer to the current
directory.

4.4 Deleting files

Before we continue, enter the following command:

```
$ cd ..
$
```

This brings us back to the "old" directory.

We copied all our text files to the directory "texts". The originals of these copies are still in the old directory. We will delete these files now. The command for this is "rm". With this command we can delete (remove) single files or several files.

```
$ rm sample
$ rm part1 text2
$
```

The first rm-command delets the file "sample". The second rm-command deletes the files "part1" and "text2". With command "ls" we can check our work and we find that the old files are actually removed.

```
$ ls
copy   texts
```

As you can see, our present directory has only two entries left, a normal file (copy) and a directory (texts).

4.5 Deleting directories

It is possible to delete directories. Command "rm" does not work for this, though. To remove a directory command "rmdir" (remove directory) has to be used.

A precondition for the removal of a directory is that the directory is empty. For that reason, we cannot remove the directory "texts". Let's try and see what happens:

```
$ rmdir texts
rmdir: texts not empty
$
```

The UNIX system tells us that the directory "texts"
is not empty. We will create an empty directory for
our experiments.

```
$ mkdir empty
$ ls
copy   empty   texts
$ rmdir empty
$ ls
copy   texts
$
```

As shown above we created a directory named "empty"
and then deleted this directory.
There is a command which allows you even to delete
directories along with their contents. You should be
very careful when using this command. This command
is "rm -r".


```
$ mkdir full
$ cp copy full/copy
$ rm full
rm: full directory
$ rm -r full
$
```

As you can see command "rm" with option "-r" removes
the (not empty) directory.

4.6 Moving files

In the section above, we first copied some files to
a new location and then deleted the original files.
Had we used command "mv" instead of command "cp" we
could have saved the work with the deletions. Let's
copy our last normal file to the directory "texts"
and at the same time delete the original:

```
$ mv copy texts/copy
$
```

Let's check the result:

```
$ ls
texts
$ ls texts
sample  copy  part1  text2
$
```

As you can see from the example above it is possible
to enter a directory as the parameter for the "ls"
command. This shows us a listing of the files in the
directory specified.

Command "mv" can also be used to rename files.

```
$ cd texts
$ mv copy text1
$ ls
sample  part1  text1  text2
$
```

As you can see "copy" has been renamed to "text1".
The moving of files is actually just a renaming
anyway.

Every file has its own pathname. When we moved the
file "copy" to the directory "texts" we did nothing
but rename the file from "/usr/elcomp/copy" to
"/usr/elcomp/texts/copy".

4.7 Read-, write-, and execution-protection

UNIX has a unique way to protect files from
unauthorized access. Each file in UNIX has its so-
called protection settings which define who can read
the file, who can change it (write), and who can
execute it. These settings can be seen if you use
command "ls" with option "-l".

```
$ ls -l
total 1
drwxr-xr-x 2 elcomp          112 Aug 20 09:30 texts
$
```

On your screen you will get a different listing.

The settings are coded in the first word.
The second word (number) indicates how many links
there are to this file. Next is the owner of the
file, followed by the size of the file (number of
characters), followed by a date indicating when the
file was changed last, followed by the name of the
file.

Now to the protection settings.
The first letter (d) there shows us that it is a
directory. The nine characters that follow can be
separated into three groups of three characters
each. The first group (rwx in our case) shows the
rights of the owner of the file.

The second group (r-x) shows the rights of the user
group to which the owner of the directory belongs.

The third group (r-x) shows the rights of all UNIX
users.

An "r" stands for "reading allowed". A "w" stands
for "writing/changing allowed". An "x" stands for
"execution allowed".

In our example, the owner of the directory can read
the directory and also write to it. He has also the
right to execute commands that might be stored in
this directory.

The UNIX users (we are part of them) have only read
allowance and execution allowance, there is no write
allowance (missing "w").

The group which the owner of the directory belongs
to has the same rights as the UNIX users.

Summary:
Protection settings use letters. If a letter is missing (minus sign instead of the letter) this indicates a missing allowance.

Let's change the directory now:

```
$ cd texts
$ ls -l
total 9
-rw-r--r-- 1 elcomp        673 Aug 20 09:28 sample
-rw-r--r-- 1 elcomp        187 Aug 20 09:28 part1
-rw-r--r-- 1 elcomp        673 Aug 20 09:30 text1
-rw-r--r-- 1 elcomp       1572 Aug 20 09:28 text2
$
```

As you can see all files are normal files, no directories. We also see that all users can read the files but not change them. We, as the owner of the files, can do both (read and write).

How do you define those settings?
Command "chmode" (change mode) allows us to do that.

Our first example removes the setting which allows users other than those of your own group to read the file.

```
$ chmode o-r text1
$
```

Now the file "text1" can no longer be read by other users. As you can see the chmode-command has two parameters. The first parameter defines what should happen to the settings. The second parameter defines the file. The "o" in the first parameter stands for "other" users, the minus sign stands for "remove", and the "r" stands for "read allowance".

In the next example we give the right to write to the file "text1" to the users of our own group.

```
$ chmod g+w text1
$
```

46

As you can see, with this example we use a "g" for "group". The "o" in the previous example stands for "other". The plus sign stands for "add". The "w" stands for "write allowance".

We can use this command to remove some of our own rights, for example to prevent inadvertent changes or deletions of a certain file.

```
$ chmod -w sample
$
```

The file "sample" can no longer be changed by the user himself. As you can see, the minus sign without a definition of a group refers to the owner of the file. If we now try to delete this file we will get a warning by the system. If we enter a "y" there, the file can be deleted nevertheless. If we just press Return, the file remains unharmed. The following examples demonstrate this:

```
$ rm sample
rm: sample 444 mode
```

Press the Return key now.

```
$
```

If you enter "ls" now:

```
$ ls
sample  part1   text1   text2
$
```

You can see that the file "sample" was not deleted.

If we enter a "y" before we press Return, the file "sample" will be deleted.

```
$ rm sample
rm: sample 444 mode y
$ ls
part1   text1   text2
$
```

The number (444 in this example) indicates the
settings in a coded form.

Let's take a look at the changes we made. We can do
that with command "ls" and the "-l" option:

```
$ ls -l
total 7
-rw-r--r-- 1 elcomp         187 Aug 20 09:28 part1
-rw-r--r-- 1 elcomp         673 Aug 20 09:30 text1
-rw-r--r-- 1 elcomp        1572 Aug 20 09:28 text2
$
```

The setting "execution allowance" will be described
later on.

Now we want to check whether these settings really
work the way they are supposed to.

```
$ cd /usr/games
$ ls -l
total 299
-rwx--x--x 1 bin      10586 Oct  1 00:00 arithmetic
-rwx--x--x 1 bin      15072 Oct  1 00:00 banner
-rwx--x--x 1 bin       8702 Oct  1 00:00 hangman
drwxrwxrwx 2 bin         96 Apr 17 19:27 lib
-rwx--x--x 1 bin       7812 Oct  1 00:00 master
-rwxr-xr-x 1 bin       7950 Oct  1 00:00 quiz
drwxrwxrwx 2 bin        544 Apr 17 19:28 quiz.k
-rwx--x--x 1 bin       7170 Oct  1 00:00 random
$ cat arithmetic
cat: can't open arithmetic
$ chmod o+r arithmetic
chmod: can't change arithmetic
$ cd
$ cd texts
$
```

This example shows us two things:
First, the protection settings work the way they are
supposed to.
Second, you obviously can change only the settings
of your own files and directories. In the example
above, the owner of the file "arithmetic" is the
user with the i.d. "bin".

4.8 How to organize your home directory

Your home directory is the directory you are in
after logging in. In our case, this is the directory
/usr/elcomp.

There is an agreement among UNIX users on how to
organize one's directories. Every user creates his
own directory system under the home directory.

Most directory systems contain the following
subdirectories:

    bin (a directory for commands, see next chapter)
    public (a directory accessible to everybody)
    other directories

Other directories can be, for example, directories
with the names of the users, if there are several
users with the same user i.d.

Every subdirectory can have other subdirectories. It
is recommended that you have directories for each
type of data, for example, a directory with all the
text files, another directory with all BASIC
programs, etc. If that is not structured enough you
can have more subdirectories, for example, two
subdirectories under the subdirectory "texts", one
with letters, the other one with other text files.

Now let's prepare our home directory.

```
$ cd
$ mkdir bin
$ mkdir public
$ chmod a+w public
$ chmod og-rx bin
$ ls -l
total 3
drwx------ 2 elcomp        32 Jul 20 13:44 bin
drwxrwxrwx 2 elcomp        32 Jul 20 13:44 public
drwxr-xr-x 2 elcomp       112 Jul 20 11:40 texts
$
```

We created a directory which can be read by everybody and written to by everybody, and, if it contains commands, these commands can be executed by everybody. The "a" in the "chmod" command stands for "all". The name of this directory is "public".

The directory "bin" is made inaccessible to everyone except ourself ("o"=others, "g"=group).

4.9 Special files

As mentioned earlier, there is a third type of file in UNIX, the so-called special files. This type of file actually is not a file; it is a device, which is treated like a file by UNIX. Your keyboard or your monitor, for example, are treated like files by UNIX.

We can read these special files or write to them.
Where do we find these files?
All devices are in the directory "/dev" and each device has its own name.
You can check what name your terminal has with the following command:

```
$ tty
/dev/tty5
$
```

The user "elcomp" works on device "tty5". Now let's enter command "ls -l" to check the permission settings for this file.

```
$ ls -l /dev/tty5
crw--w--w- 1 elcomp   0, 0 Jul 20 14:53 /dev/tty5
$
```

The "c" stands for "character type file". As you can see everybody is allowed to write to this file, but nobody can read it.

The Shell

5

This name has nothing to do with the Shell oil company. It describes a shell around the kernal of UNIX. It is the device we use to communicate with the kernal.

All commands that we executed so far (except the editor commands) were Shell commands. We entered the commands, and the Shell executed the commands using the UNIX operating system. The Shell is not just a command interpreter, but it is a programming language in itself.

5.1 Abbreviations for files

The Shell allows you to use abbreviations for file names. We use so-called wildcard characters for that.

The following example shows the use of the asterisk ("*").

```
$ cd texts
$ ls tex*
text1   text2
$ ls *1
part1   text1
$
```

The asterisk stands for "any character". The asterisk can be anywhere in the name. There can be more than one asterisk in one word.

Another wildcard character is the question mark. Some examples of this:

```
$ ls text?
text1  text2
$ ls ????1
part1  text1
$ ls ???t?
part1  text1  text2
$
```

As you can see, the question mark stands for "any character" also, but only for one character, while the asterisk can be no character, one character, or several characters.

In the first example, all files with a name starting with "tex" and ending with any character are listed.

5.2 Input and output with the Shell

Almost any command involves input and output of data. The "ls" command, for example, has a listing of files as its output. The "cat" command needs the name of a file as input and sends the contents of the file as output.

If no destination is defined for the output, the UNIX standard output device, which is the screen, is used. So far, we took it for granted that all output goes to the screen, but the output can go to another file as well. How this is done is shown below:

```
$ ls > lsout
$
```

The output of the "ls" command now is in the file "lsout". We can check that with the "cat" command:

```
$ cat lsout
bin  lsout  public  texts
$
```

The character ">" allows us to redirect an output.

We can do something similar with the input:

```
$ cat < lsout
bin  lsout  public  texts
$
```

The "cat" command uses the file "lsout" as its input
now. As you can see the input can be redirected with
the character "<".

In this example the command without the character
"<" would have accomplished the same.

The character ">" followed by a file name erases the
old contents of the file if a file with this name
already exists. Sometimes we don't want this to
happen. There is a solution to this in UNIX. If the
character ">>" is used instead of ">", the output is
appended to the data already in the file. Example:

```
$ ls texts >> lsout
$ cat lsout
bin  lsout  public  texts  part1  text1  text2
$
```

As you can see the output has been appended to the
existing data in the file "lsout".

Each command has a second output: the error messages
(if any occur). We can redirect this output as well:

```
$ cat file 2> error
$ cat error
cat: can't open file
$
```

As you can see, the command "2>" allows us to
redirect the output of error messages. The "2"
stands for the second output channel.

The redirection of the input also has another
version:

```
$ cat << EOF
> These two lines will appear
> again on the screen
> EOF
These two lines will appear
again on the screen
$
```

The character "<<" means that the input has to be
taken directly from the keyboard. The end of the
input is defined by the string following this
character. As you can see the prompt changes during
input. The character ">" as a prompt indicates that
a Shell command is not completed yet.

5.3 Connecting input and output of different commands (piping)

A unique feature of UNIX, the so-called piping,
allows you to use the output of one command directly
as the input of another command. The character "|"
is used to connect two commands in that way.
Example:

```
$ cd texts
$ cat text2 | wc
     30     228     1572
$
```

The output of the "cat" command (the contents of the
file "text2") is used as the input to the command
"wc" (word count). This command determines the
number of lines, words, and characters in a file.

It is possible to connect more than two commands in
the manner described. That way you can construct
filter commands that hand over only certain parts of

their input. Our next example uses a filter command.
This "grep" command will be described more detailed
in a later chapter.

```
$ cat copy | grep editor | sort
Although this editor is a so-called line oriented editor
The answer to this is, that the editor allows you to write data,
The editor is called with "ed", usually followed by a file name.
UNIX standard editor.
editor first of all.
$
```

The result of the above command sequence is an
output of an alphabetically sorted list of all lines
containing the word "editor".

5.4 Entering several commands in one line

The Shell allows us to enter more than one command
in one line. The different commands have to
separated by a semicolon (";").

```
$ ls ; cat part1
copy            crpt               lpr              mbox              outp
part1           prlpr              sample           text2
The UNIX edit?r "ed"

The editor is called with "ed", usually followed by a FILE name.
This line was changed with the change command.
This text contains typos.
$
```

As you can see first the files in the directory are
listed, and then the contents of the file "part1"
are listed. If you want to enter more commands than
would fit on one line, you can enter a backslash
("\") at the end of the line and continue on the
next line. Example:

```
$ cat part1 text2 | grep editor | sort | uniq | grep is | sort | uniq \
> | wc
      4      46       252
$
```

This extremely long sequence of commands determines
the number of lines that are different and contain
the words "editor" and "is" as well as the number of
words and characters in these three lines.

When you enter this sequence of commands and reach
the second line (after the backslash was entered),
the prompt ">" will be displayed, indicating that
the input is not finished yet.

Now to the main subject of this chapter: how
commands can be put together.

```
$ (cat part1 ; echo "And now with grep" ;
cat part1 ! grep with) > cat+grep
$ cat cat+grep
The UNIX edit?r "ed"

The editor is called with "ed", usually followed by a FILE name.
This line was changed with the change command.
This text contains typos.
And now with grep
The editor is called with "ed", usually followed by a FILE name.
This line was changed with the change command.
$
```

The commands between parentheses are put together
into one command. This put together command has one
common output. The use of this will become clear in
the next chapter.

Another command, command "echo" is used in this
example. This command just sends its parameters to
the standard output device.

5.5 Background processing of commands

There are commands that take so much time to execute
that it can become boring if you have to wait for
the command to finish, and the computer cannot be
used for anything else during this time. This may be
the case with many operating systems, but not with
UNIX. UNIX allows you to let commands work in the
background while you can do something else in the
foreground.

This means you can enter a command, and move it to
the background so that you don't have to wait for
the command to finish before you can enter another
command. The character "&" is used to indicate that
you want a command to be executed in the background.

Example:


```
$ (cat * | grep editor | grep is | sort | uniq) > outp &
43
$ cat outp
$ cat outp
Although this editor is a so-called line oriented editor
The answer to this is, that the editor allows you to write data,
The editor is called with "ed", usually followed by a FILE name.
The editor is called with "ed", usually followed by a file name.
$
```


After you have entered the sequence of commands, followed by a "&", a number will be displayed on the screen. This is the so-called UNIX process number. We will talk about the term "process" a little later on. The "cat" commands in the above example show that we are back in the Shell right after we enter the command. Both "cat" commands display the contents of the file that is created in the background. After the first of the two commands, the file "outp" seems to be empty. After the second command, the background process obviously is finished and the file contains data. When you try this, it might be different; you might get a listing the first time you enter the "cat" command or the third or fourth time. This depends on how your system is utilized at the time you do this.

5.6 Shell programs

As was mentioned earlier, the Shell is not just a command interpreter, but it also allows you to write structured programs. These programs can be saved as new commands on disk. The Shell thus allows you to combine existing commands to form new ones. The example listed below prints a file on the printer together with the date and the page number.

We use the editor to create our program.

```
$ ed prlpr
?prlpr
a
pr $1 | lp
.
w
12
q
$ chmod +x prlpr
$ prlpr text1
$
```

The new command consists of a "pr" command (prints a file and on each new page it prints the date, the name of the file and the page number) and a "lp" command (prints a file on a printer). The dollar sign with the "1" represents a variable. This variable stands for the first parameter (that's the 1) that is entered together with the command.

Once the program has been created, we have to change its permission setting so that it can be executed (the "x"). After this is done, we check whether the command works the way we want it. If everything is o.k. the printout should look as follows:

```
User: Elcomp                                          Page  1
Tue Oct  9 19:21:58 1984




part1     Oct  9 19:21 1984   Last mod: Nov  1 13:12 1984    Page 1

The UNIX edit?r "ed"

The editor is called with "ed", usually followed by a FILE name.
This line was changed with the change command.
This text contains typos.
```

5.7 The Shell variables

As you have seen in the above program, a Shell program can contain variables. This is not only true for a program, but also for the normal Shell environment.

Every Shell contains some important variables. Command "set" shows which variables are defined with your system.

```
    $ set
    HOME=/usr/elcomp
    IFS=

    PATH=:/bin:/usr/bin
    PS1=$
    PS2=>
    SHELL=/bin/sh
    TERM=alt2
    $
```

As you can see, some variables have already been defined.

HOME
defines which directory is the home directory. This is the directory you get to when you enter a plain "cd". After logging in your are in your home directory.

IFS
displays the separating characters. We can't see them in the listing because they are the space, the Tab, and the Return.

PATH
This variable shows you the directories where the different commands are stored. The different directories shown are separated by colons.

PS1
contains the first Shell prompt. The standard prompt is the Dollar sign, but you may change that.

PS2
contains the second prompt. This prompt can be changed as well.

SHELL
shows which Shell we are in. Besides the normal
Shell "sh", there are other Shells such as "csh", a
Shell which has great similarities to the language
C, or "bsh", a business oriented Shell.

TERM
shows the terminal type used.

You probably noticed that all variables are written
with capitals. It is usual with UNIX to write all
variables with capitals. On your system, you may
obtain more variables with the "set" command. These
variables have a special meaning on your system.

As we have seen in our example (prlpr), there are
other variables. These variables refer to the
parameters that are handed over to the Shell or to
the program when the command is called.

Variables are marked by a preceding dollar sign. In
our example we used "$1". This refers to the first
parameter entered together with the command. There
can be more variables like this: "$2","$3", etc.

$# refers to the number of parameters.

Let's define some variables now:

```
$ a="this is the value of variable a"
$ echo $a
this is the value of variable a
$
```

As you can see, a value is assigned to a variable
through the equation sign. Using the "echo" command
we can display the value of the variable. If we
assign a new value to the variable, the old value
will be overwritten.

```
$ a="new value"
$ echo $a
new value
$
```

The following example shows how new values can be
added to the existing ones:

```
    $ a=$a" and totally new value"
    $ echo $a
    new value and totally new value
    $
```

It is possible to assign commands to a variable. In
this case the command has to be between "`"
characters (not "'" characters !).

```
    $ a=`tty`
    $ b='tty'
    $ echo $a
    /dev/tty5
    $ echo $b
    tty
    $
```

As you can see, variable "a" contains the "tty"
command now. The "tty" command shows which terminal
we are currently working on. Variable "b" is not
interpreted as a command, but as the string "tty"
because the wrong characters have been used.

Now enter the following:

```
    $ $b
    /dev/tty5
    $
```

This time the "tty" command has been executed. The
variable "b" has the value "tty".

Before we define new variables, we change the path
for the commands. We do that with the following
command:

```
    $ PATH=.:/usr/elcomp/bin:/bin:/usr/bin:/usr/games
    $ echo $PATH
    .:/usr/elcomp/bin:/bin:/usr/bin:/usr/games
    $ export PATH
    $
```

The "export" command defines that the variable PATH has the same value in sub-shells and in Shell programs. If we had not done that, the change of the variable would only be valid locally. You should know that with each call a "new" shell is used. When the command is finished, the shell is left. This makes it possible to use local variables.

The period in the listing above could have been left out, it refers to the current directory. That means the command is first searched for in the current directory. If it cannot be found there, it is searched for in "/usr/elcomp/bin", next in "/bin", "/usr/bin", and "/usr/games". The path defines the sequence in which to search. If the command cannot be found in any of those directories, an error message "not found" will be displayed.

For the next examples, it is better to go to a different directory:

```
$ cd ../bin
$ pwd
/usr/elcomp/bin
$
```

5.8 Control structures in the Shell

Just like a real programming language, the Shell has its own control structures. These are even better than the ones used in the popular programming language BASIC.

Control structure means elements of the language that make decisions based on logical conditions. An example of a control structure is the "if-then-else" structure. The Shell has other additional structures, like "while-do-done", "for do done", "case in".

All these structures are described in this chapter, but first some words about the so-called logical

conditions. A logical condition can only have one of
two values: "true", or "false". In the Shell, "true"
is represented by a zero; "false" is represented by
a number different than zero. Every command delivers
a value. This value is "true" if the command was
executed without error, and "false" if an error
occurred.

5.8.1 Command "test"

Command "test" checks a command and delivers the
result "true" or "false". This command allows you to
check whether a string is empty, whether a file is a
normal file or a directory, etc. Below is a survey
of the different possibilities the "test" command
gives you:

```
test -r file  true if "file" exists and is readable
test -w file  true if "file" exists and is writeable
test -f file  true if "file" exists and is not a
                    directory
test -d file  true if "file" exists and is a
                    directory
test -s file  true if "file" exists and has more
                    than 0 characters
test -z string  true if length of "string" is 0
test -n string  true if length of "string" is > 0
test s1=s2  true if string "s1" is equal string "s2"
test s1!=s2  true if string "s1" is not equal
                  string "s2"
test string  true if "string" is not empty
test n1 -eq n2  true if the integers n1 and n2 are
                  equal. -eq can be replaced by:
                  -ne  not equal
                  -gt  greater
                  -ge  greater or equal
                  -lt  less than
                  -le  less or equal
```

The above expressions can be combined with the
following operators:

```
!   not operator, true becomes false and vice versa
-a  logical AND function, true if both are true
```

-o logical OR function, true if one is true
(expr) parentheses for combination of expressions

We will talk about some of these functions in more
detail in later chapters.

5.8.2 The IF instruction

Format:

```
if <condition>
then <list of commands>
else <list of commands>
fi
```

If the condition is true (zero) then the list of
commands   following   "then"   will   be   executed,
otherwise the list of commands following "else" will
be executed. The command "else" and the list of
commands following it can be omitted. The words
"if", "then", and "else" should be placed on new
lines. These commands are recognized only if they
follow a Return, or a semicolon (";").

Enter the following example now:

```
$ ed ex1
?ex1
a
if { read n1
     read n2
     test $n1 -eq $n2
   }
then echo $n1 "is equal" $n2
else if test $n1 -lt $n2
     then echo $n2 "is greater than" $n2
     else echo $n2 "is less than" $n1
     fi
fi
.
w
199
q
$ chmod +x ex1
$ ex1
```

If you have entered all that, the Shell program will ask for the input of two numbers (read n1 and read n2). Enter for example these two numbers:

    1234
    1034
    1034 is less than 1234
    $

The program has answered us. If we enter a character instead of a number, the program assumes a value of zero for the character. The braces ("{" and "}") are needed only if there is a list of commands (more than one command). The "if" instruction itself is delimited by the words "if" and "fi".

5.8.3 The WHILE instruction

Format:

```
while <condition>
do
    <list of commands>
done
```

The list of commands delimited by "do" and "done" is executed until the condition becomes false.

An example of the use of such a loop is shown below:

```
$ ed ex2
$ex2
a
while {
        read a
        test "$a" != "end"
        }
 do
```

```
    echo $a
done
.
w
78
q
$ chmod +x ex2
$ ex2
hello this is a test
hello this is a test
bye bye
bye bye
end
$
```

As you can see, each input is repeated (echo $a)
until we enter the word "end".
WHILE...DO loops can be nested.

5.8.4 The UNTIL instruction

Format:

```
until <condition>
do
    <list of commands>
done
```

The UNTIL instruction is very similar to the WHILE
instruction. The difference is, that here the list
of commands is executed until the condition becomes
true. This is shown by changing the previous example
slightly:

```
$ ed ex3
?ex3
a
until {
        read a
        test "$a = "end"
        }
```

```
do
    echo $a
done
.
w
76
q
$ chmod +x ex3
$ ex3
This program does the same as ex2
This program does the same as ex2
but an until-loop is used instead of a while-loop
but an until-loop is used instead of a while-loop
end
$
```

5.8.5 The FOR instruction

Format:

```
for <variable> in <list of words>
do
    <list of commands>
done
```

The FOR instruction does not have a condition. For
that reason, it is also called an unconditioned
loop. The loop is run through until the last
variable in the list of words has been used. A
"word" in this case can be a real word or a
variable. Variables are preceded by a dollar sign.

Wildcard characters are allowed in words. In this
case, all names that can be constructed out of this
word are used.

Instead of:

```
for i in $1 $2 $3 $4 .... etc.
do
    something
done
```

you can also use:

```
    for i
    do
        something
    done
```

The variable "i" uses all parameters in both cases.
The second way of writing it has the advantage that
it does not use empty parameters.

Example:

```
$ ed ex4
?ex4
a
for i in "contents of current directory" *
do
   echo $i
done
.
w
61
q
$ chmod +x ex4
$ ex4
contents of current directory
cat+grep
copy
crpt
ex4
lpr
mbox
outp
part1
prlpr
sample
text2
$
```

We have written a new "ls" command now. The asterisk
is used as a wildcard character here.

5.8.6 The CASE instruction

Format:

```
    case <variable> in
         <pattern 1> ) <list of commands> ;;
         <pattern 2> ) <list of commands> ;;
                      :
                      :
         <pattern n> ) <list of commands> ;;
    esac
```

The CASE instruction checks whether the variable
corresponds to a certain pattern. If this is the
case, then the matching set of commands is executed.
Patterns can contain wildcard characters. If the
variable corresponds with more than one pattern, the
list of commands belonging to the first pattern will
be executed.

Example:

```
$ ed ex5
?ex5
a
case $1 in
-ls ) ls -l $2 ;;
-cat) cat $2 ;;
*    ) echo "Usage ex5 <-ls> file or ex5 <-cat> file"
esac
.
w
103
q
$ chmod +x ex5
$ ex5 -ls ex5
-rwxrwxr-x 1 elcomp      103 Oct  9 19:50 ex5
$ ex5 -cat ex5
case $1 in
-ls ) ls -l $2 ;;
-cat) cat $2 ;;
*    ) echo "Usage ex5 <-ls> file or ex5 <-cat> file"
esac
$ ex5 blabla
Usage ex5 <-ls> file or ex5 <-cat> file
$
```

Our sample program executes either an "ls" command or a "cat" command. The first parameter ($1) determines which command is selected. If no parameter or a wrong parameter is used, an error message will result. The name of the file has to be entered as the second parameter along with the command.

For more examples, check in the matching chapters.

5.9 The ".profile"

A unique Shell program is the one called ".profile". This program is in the home directory of a every user. This program is executed when a user logs in. This program in most cases already exists in your directory. This program normally sets variables. You may check whether there is a ".profile" file in your directory with the following command:

```
SUPER> cd
SUPER> ls -a
.                   ..                  .profile        cale        cals
checklist           cron                dead.letter     getty       group
init                mkfs                mknod           motd        mount
mtab                passwd              rc              termcap     ttys
umount              utmp                wall
SUPER>
```

As you can see, there are other files you probably didn't know about before. The option "-a" in the "ls" command shows us all these "invisible" files. All these files are preceded by a period. On your system there are the two files marked "." and ".."; the other files depend on the system you are on; there may be different files on your system than the ones listed above. The file named "." contains the current directory. The file named ".." contains the father directory of the current directory.

Let's take a closer look at ".profile" now:

```
$ cat .profile
stty erase kill
$
```

Your ".profile" file probably contains different information. In our case, the keys for deleting a character and a line are defined.

Let's add the PATH command (displays path for commands) to that:

```
$ ed .profile
20
a
PATH=.:/usr/elcomp/bin:/bin:/usr/bin:/usr/games
.
w
68
q
$
```

On your system, you will get a different number here. If there was no ".profile" file on your system, you have to make the file we just created executable. This is done as follows:

```
$ chmod +x .profile
$
```

NOTES

6

PROCESSES

We already talked about a process in a previous chapter. We talked about commands (programs) that work in the background. A process is nothing but a command (program) that is being executed. Inside UNIX, many such processes are running at the same time. In order to distinguish between the different processes, each process gets its number.

Every process has been started by another process. This process is called the father process. In UNIX processes are numbered with increasing numbers, so that the father process always has a lower number than the son. The first process is the one with number zero, and it is the one that is started first. The process with number one is the father of all the other processes. Every user can start a process. With the "ps" command you can look at your processes:

```
$ ps
   PID TTY  TIME CMD
    52 5    0:01 ps
$
```

What does this output mean?
The number in column "PID" is the process number (Process IDentification). The number in the column "TTY" is the terminal number from which the process was started. In column "TIME" the time needed for the process so far is displayed. In the last column ("CMD") the name of the process (command) is displayed.

As you can see, every command we enter obviously is
a process.
If we start a process in the background and enter
the "ps" command again now, we can see the command
in the process list:

```
    $ sleep 40 &
    56
    $ ps
       PID TTY   TIME CMD
        56 5     0:00 sleep 40
        57 5     0:02 ps
    $
```

Command "sleep" lets a process sleep for a while, 40
seconds in our example. Since we let this command
run in the background, we can continue with the
input. This example doesn't have a practical meaning
of course, but it shows the meaning of a process. If
we enter command "ps" a while later, we can see that
the "sleep" command is no longer in the list, which
means it has been finished.

```
    $ ps
       PID TTY   TIME CMD
        59 5     0:01 ps
    $
```

Besides our own processes, we can check all other
processes currently running under the UNIX system.
The command for this is as follows:

```
    $ ps -ax
       PID TTY   TIME CMD
         0 ?     40:21 swapper
         1 ?      0:02 /etc/init
        18 co     0:01 /etc/update
        20 co     0:00 /etc/cron
        26 co     0:00 setmode /dev/tty6 1200
        27 co     0:01 -sh
        37 co     0:01 leave
        50 co     0:03 ed chapter6
        41 5      0:00 -sh
```

```
   61 5     0:04 ps -ax
   28 2     0:00 - 2 (getty)
   29 3     0:00 - 2 (getty)
   30 4     0:00 - 2 (getty)
$
```

The "a" means we want to see all commands presently
running that were started from a terminal. The "x"
means we also want to see commands that were not
started from a terminal. On your terminal you will
get a completely different list from the one shown
above. In the example above there is one process,
the one numbered zero, which obviously is running
since the system was booted. This swap process is
very important in UNIX. It is the process that makes
it possible to run several processes at the same
time. This process loads the other processes into
the computer's memory, where they are executed for a
while. After a certain period of time, which is
determined by another important process, the process
is stored at the disk at its current state and
another process is loaded into memory.

The process which controls all that is process
number one (/etc/init). This process started the
process management and other important processes.

One of these processes is the process "/etc/update".
As the name indicates, this process assures that
everything is stored on disk in its latest form.

Another important process is the process "cron".
This process manages commands that have to be
executed at a certain time, for example "at"
commands.

We also see our own "ps" command and another command
which obviously was assigned to us. This is the
Shell process. Every user gets such a process
assigned to him. Without this process a user would
not be able to execute commands.

There also is another user on the system. This user

works on terminal (TTY) "co". This refers to the console. It is the terminal which communicates with the system first. This terminal belongs to the system operator. It looks like he is just now using the editor. There are also processes linked to other terminals, but nobody is logged in there. These terminals send out a "login:" and wait for the input of user i.d. and password. If both are entered correctly, the user gets a Shell-process assigned to him.

Command "ps" has an option which displays a longer output. Example:

```
$ ps -1
Tue Oct  9 18:49    Free Core = 120.5Kb,  Swap = 0/750 blks,  Procs = 4/25

USER   TTY    PID PRI NICE S(Kb) FLAGS  STATUS    USR% SYS% COMMAND
root          0-100   0   1.0          swapping   0.0  0.0 swapper
root          1  40   0  12.0          waiting    0.0  0.0
elcomp co     13 40   0  13.0   T      waiting    0.0  0.0 -sh
 *     co     14 90 -10  19.5   T      running    0.0  0.0 ps -1

$
```

With this option we get the whole process status. We cannot describe the complete list here. Interesting for us is just the column PPID (Parent Process ID). This tells us about the father process of a certain process. In our case this is number 41. This is correct, as you can see, in the previous output, where the Shell process assigned to us has the number 41.

6.1 Kill a process

This is less cruel than it might sound. It is possible to stop a process in progress, if the need for that should arise. For example, if a process got out of control.

Command "kill" needs a signal number as its first parameter. The other parameter(s) are one or several process numbers. The signal number defines which signal should be sent to the process. An immediate termination is indicated by a "-9".

For demonstration of the "kill" command we enter the
following example:

```
$ while true
> do sleep 1
> done &
197
$ ps
   PID TTY  TIME CMD
   210 5     0:02 ps
   216 5     0:00  (sleep)
$
```

This example generates sleep commands in   the
background. The father process of these sleep-
commands is process number 197. This process is not
listed in the normal process list,   we can only see
it if we call the extended version of the process
list.

Let's kill this meaningless process now.

```
$ kill -9 197
197 killed
$ ps
   PID TTY  TIME CMD
   269 5     0:01 ps
$
```

As you can see, process number 197 has been stopped.
We can also check that with command "ps".

6.2 Processes continue after a UNIX session

If you log out of the system, all processes that you
have started are stopped. The logging out happens
with command Ctrl-D.

When you finish your session, all processes whose
father you were are sent a hangup signal. After that
all processes are stopped.

If you don't want that to happen, you can use a
command which avoids that. This command is "nohup"
(no hangup). Example:

```
$ nohup sleep 300 &
22
$ Sending output to 'nohup.out'
ps
Tue Oct  9 18:52     Free Core = 106.0Kb,   Swap = 0/750 blks,   Procs = 5/25

USER  TTY    PID PRI NICE S(Kb) FLAGS   STATUS      USR% SYS% COMMAND
elcomp co     13  40    0  12.5   T     waiting      0.0  0.0 -sh
  *    co     22  90    5  16.0         snoozing     0.0  0.0 sleep 300
  *    co     25  91  -10  18.5   T     running      0.0  0.0 ps

$ ^D
login: elcomp
Password:
Welcome to VENIX          Tue Oct  9 18:53:08 1984
      VenturCom's VENIX/86 Revision 1.18
$ ps
Tue Oct  9 18:53     Free Core = 105.5Kb,   Swap = 0/750 blks,   Procs = 5/25

USER  TTY    PID PRI NICE S(Kb) FLAGS   STATUS      USR% SYS% COMMAND
elcomp co     26  40    0  13.0   T     waiting      0.0  0.0 -sh
  *    co     27  91  -10  18.5   T     running      0.0  0.0 ps
elcomp co     22  90    5  16.0         snoozing     0.0  0.0 sleep 300

$
```

As you can see the process "sleep 300" is still
there after logging out and in again.

When we entered the process with the "nohup"
command, we got a message telling us that the output
of the command is being sent to the file
"nohup.out".

UNIX as a post office

7

UNIX allows us to communicate electronically. There are two ways of communication between the users of UNIX. The first is more like making a phone call; the second is rather like sending a letter.

7.1 The "write" command

Command "write" allows direct communication between two UNIX users. Both users have to be logged in. You may check which users are logged in with command "who":

```
$ who
floegel     tty2      Aug 24 08:03
frank       tty3      Aug 24 08:05
hofacker    tty4      Aug 24 08:01
elcomp      tty5      Aug 24 08:21
wagner      tty6      Aug 24 08:19
$
```

As you can see, there are five users logged in. Command "who" also shows which terminal each user is using and at what time they logged in. If we want to send a message to user frank, we have to enter the following:

```
$ write frank
Hello Frank,
if you have time tonight, we can
have a drink at Baxters.
What do you think about that?

Greetings, Bill
<CTRL-D>
$
```

On user frank's screen the following will appear:

    Message from elcomp tty5...
    Hello Frank,
    if you have time tonight, we can
    have a drink at Baxters.
    What do you think about that?

    Greetings, Bill
    EOF

If not specified otherwise, command "write" expects
an input from the keyboard. It is possible to create
a file containing our message and use this file as
the input to the "write" command (character "<").

Most   of   the   time command "write"   is   used
interactively, that means the message is entered
directly into the terminal when it is sent.   The
advantage of this is, that the receiver can answer
right away and you answer him, etc., so that a real
dialogue is happening.

When you are in a dialogue, it is important to know
when your partner has finished his sentence and it
is your turn to answer. The example below shows how
this is handled:

        user elcomp   user frank
        ___________   __________

$ write frank   message from elcomp tty5.
Hello Frank, if you have   Hello Frank, if you have
time tonight, we can   time tonight, we can
have a drink at Baxters.   have a drink at Baxters.
What do you think about   What do you think about
that?   that?
-o-   -o-

message from frank tty3.   write elcomp
Sounds good to me. Will   Sounds good to me. Will
you pick me up ?   you pick me up ?
-o-   -o-

80

user elcomp	**user frank**

```
I come over at 7 p.m.        I come over at 7 p.m.
is that O.K. with you ?      is that O.K. with you ?
-o-                          -o-

Yes that is perfect.         Yes that is perfect.
See you then.                See you then.
-o+o-                        -o+o-
EOF                          <Ctrl-D>

See you later, Frank !       See you later, Frank !
-o+o-                        -o+o-
<Ctrl-D>                     EOF
$
```

The "-o-" means "over", it indicates the end of the
sentence. The "-o+o-" means "over and out", it means
that you want to end the communication. The <Ctrl-D>
at the end actually terminates the communication.

If you don't wish to be disturbed by messages, you
can use command "mesg" as follows:

```
$ mesg n
$
```

If you try to send a message to user frank now, the
following will happen:

```
$ write frank

Permission denied
$
```

This tells us that at present it is not possible to
send messages to user frank.

If user frank is ready to receive messages again, he
merely has to enter the following:

```
$ mesg y
$
```

Besides the message "Permission denied" there can be
another message. If you try to communicate with a
user who is not logged in, you will get the
following message:

```
$ write bill
bill not logged in.
$
```


7.2 Command "mail"

If you would rather send a letter to a user than to
get in a dialogue with him (maybe he is not logged
in or he doesn't want to receive messages), the
Shell offers you another way of communication.
Command "mail" allows you to send letters. The same
command is used to check your mailbox.

First we will send a letter. We can use the editor
to write the letter. The advantage of this is, that
this way we can correct the letter before sending
it, and it also leaves us with a copy of the letter.

```
$ ed letter
?letter
a
With this letter I inform you
that on:

    November 30th 1984 at 8:00 pm

in:

    55 Main Street
    Chino

a dinner will take place, in celebration of
my wife's birthday.
You are invited to that dinner.

Greetings,

    Jim Miller
.
w
248
q
$ mail smith < letter
```

As you can see the addressee is entered as with the "write" command. Since we already prepared the letter with the editor, we use command "<" to define the input file.

If you try to send a letter to a user who doesn't exist, the following message will be displayed:

        $ mail cuckoo < letter
        mail: can't send to cuckoo
        mail saved in dead.letter
        $

The system tells us that no mail can be sent to cuckoo. The letter that can not be delivered is saved in our own directory in a file called "dead.letter".

How do you know whether you got a letter?
You have to check your mailbox by entering the word "mail". If a letter is sent to you, you are not automatically notified. This is different from the "write" command. If you are logging in, the system checks your mailbox for you and notifies you if you have mail waiting for you:

        login: smith
        Password

        XENIX Version 2.5a

        You have mail.

        $

The message "You have mail" reminds you to check your mailbox. You can use command "mail" to empty your mailbox.

```
$ mail
From elcomp Tue Jul 24 09:09:17 1984
Dear Mr. Smith,
With this letter I inform you
that on:

     November 30th 1984 at 8:00 pm

in:

     55 Main Street
     Chino


a dinner will take place, in celebration of
my wife's birthday.
You are invited to that dinner.

Greetings,

     Jim Miller
```

In the first line the sender and the date and time
the mail was received, followed by the message, are
displayed. Now the command "mail" waits for the
input of a command. If you press Return, the next
letter, if there is any, will be displayed. If there
is no more mail, we leave the command, with the
letter(s) remaining.

Here is a survey of other commands available:

```
d         delete the letter just displayed
p         display mail again
-         display previous letter (if there was any)
s name    save letter in the file named
          if no name is specified, the name "mbox"
          is used. More than one name may be entered
          in order to create copies of the letter
w name    like s, but no sender information, just
          the letter itself is being saved
m user    send letter along to specified user(s)
          if no user is specified, the letter is
          sent to you again
```

q   leave the "mail" command
x   leave "mail" command without changing the
           mailbox file
! command execute the specified command
              immediately
?   display command options available

As you can see, UNIX is an operating system which
has the future in mind. In the newer versions of
UNIX the possibilities of electronic mail and
communications have been enhanced a lot. UNIX also
has software built in which allows data
communication over computer networks. Several
companies offer hard- and software for such
networks. Worth mentioning in this context is
"Teamnet II" by Altos. Through the creation of a
super-root (the mother of all other roots in the
system) the system acts as if you had an extended
file system. By entering a pathname that goes via
this super-root (indicated by "@"), it is possible
to read or change files on other computers.

NOTES

8

Organizing and sorting data in UNIX

As you already know, it is possible in UNIX to use the output of one command as the input of another command (piping).

This feature is helpful if you want to sort or filter the output of a command. It sometimes happens that you only need parts of a file, and you want to "throw away" the rest. For that there are several commands available in UNIX (grep, sort, egrep, fgrep, awk, etc.). In this chapter we will talk about two of these commands: "grep" and "sort".

The other commands are described in detail in the UNIX manuals.

8.1 The "sort" command

This command sorts an input (a file) alphabetically (lexicographically). Besides that, this command can do a lot more. Here is a survey of the different options of this command:

Format:

    sort [-bdfinr] [-tc] [+pos [-pos]] ...

Meaning of the options:

    b   leading blanks don't matter
    d   only letters, numbers, and blanks matter
    f   capitalization doesn't matter
    i   characters outside the ASCII range are ignored
    n   numbers are compared numerically
    r   reverse sort
    tc fields are separated by the character "c"

+pos and -pos define the range in a field, that should count for the sort. The fields are separated by either a blank or by the character "c" as described under the option "tc".

The numbering of the fields normally starts at zero. The number following the plus sign defines the field from where the sort should start. The number following the minus sign marks the field in front of which the comparison should end. The example below explains this:

```
$ sort -f +1 -2 part1

The editor is called with "ed", usually followed by a FILE name.
This line was changed with the change command.
This text contains typos.
The UNIX edit?r "ed"
$
```

In the above example the file "part1" is sorted as follows:

The sort key is restricted to the second and third field through "+1" and "-2".

    The /editor/ is called ...
    This /line/ was changed ...
    This /text/ contains ...

When sorting only the second field in each line is considered (see markers above).

The "-f" means that lower case and upper case are treated equally (ignore capitalization).

88

Check the file to see whether it got sorted the way
you expected it.

Our next example shows that it is possible to sort
by more than one field.


```
$ ed text3
?text3
a
Good Morning misses miller how are you today
Goot Morning misses miller how are you today
Goot Morning misses Miller how are you today
Goot Morning Misses Miller how are you today
.
w
180
q
$ sort -f +5 -7 +0 -1 +3 -4 text3
Good Morning misses miller how are you today
Goot Morning Misses Miller how are you today
Goot Morning misses Miller how are you today
Goot Morning misses miller how are you today
$
```


As you can see, several fields can be defined. The
sequence is important. The sort key always is
referred to the first field. If these fields are
equal, the key refers to the next definition. This
is repeated until no additional definition is found.
Command "sort" refers the sort key to all fields
that remained. This form of sort can be seen clearly
in our example. Here is a step by step description
of what happens in the example:

First the sort key is referred to the sixth through
the eighth field. In our example, this is the string
"are you today". This string is the same in all
lines. Next, the sort command takes the next field
definition. This refers only to the first field (+0,
-1). That means now it is sorted according to the
first field. Since "d" comes before "t" in the
alphabet, the first sentence can be printed.

The rest of the lines have to be sorted again, but
now the sort refers to the fourth field (+3,-4).
Since an "M" comes before an "m", one of the two
lines with the "M" has to become the second line. It
has to be decided between these two lines. Since no
more fields are defined, the sofar unused field with
the lowest number is used for the decision.

Field number two is the same in both sentences, so
the third field is used. Now a difference is
detected and the line with the "M" goes in front of
the line with the "m".

The file is now sorted and it is displayed on the
screen.

Besides defining fields, we can also specify
character positions within a field. The next example
shows this technique:

```
$ sort -f +0.0 -0.1 +1 -2 part1

The editor is called with "ed", usually followed by a FILE name.
This line was changed with the change command.
This text contains typos.
The UNIX edit?r "ed"
$
```

Which characters within a field should be considered
are defined by a number connected to the field
number through a period. In our example "+0.0 -0.1"
means from the first to the second character in the
first field. This means for the sort command, that
the sort key should be compared first to the very
first character in each line. In the example the
file "part1" is sorted according to the first
character in each line. In case there are two equal
characters, the second field (+1 -2) decides.

If you specify "+1.4 -3.5", the sort key is compared
to all characters from the fifth position in the
second field through the fifth character in the
fourth field.

The "sort" command is one of the most useful
commands of the Shell.

90

8.2 Command "grep"

Besides the "sort" command, which sorts a file,
there is the command "grep". This command picks
certain lines out of a file. The command looks as
follows:

Format:

    grep [-opt] [pattern] file ...

The specified file(s) are checked line by line. If
the specified pattern is found, the line will be
displayed depending on the options specified. Here
is a survey of the options available:

y   ignore capitalization, similar to "f" with "sort"
v   lines that do not contain the pattern are printed
c   only the number of lines containing the pattern
    is printed
n   the line number of the line containing the
    pattern is printed in front of the text
e   patterns starting with "-" have to be preceded
    by the "e"
l   the name of the file(s) containing the pattern
    is printed

Let's check command "grep" now, using some examples:

```
$ grep 'is' part1
The editor is called with "ed", usually followed by a FILE name.
This line was changed with the change command.
This text contains typos.
$
```

In our first example all lines containing the string
"is" are displayed. No option is needed for this.

Next let's check which lines of this file do not
contain the string "is":

```
$ grep -v 'is' part1
The UNIX edit?r "ed"

$
```

This command shows us the complementary lines of the
first example. If we also need the line numbers of
the lines found by the above command, we enter the
following:

```
$ grep -v -n 'is' sample
2:UNIX standard editor.
8:editor first of all.
$
```

The next example shows us that it is possible to
search several files with one command:

```
$ grep -v -n 'is' text*
text2:1:The UNIX edit?r "ed"
text2:2:
text2:9:Why learn the edit?r first?
text2:15:UNIX standard editor.
text2:21:editor first of all.
$
```

In this example you can see that the name of the
file is printed in front of each line (if there is
more than one file to be searched).

If we only want a display of the name of the file
containing the pattern, we use option "L":

```
$ grep -L 'is' *1
part1
text1
$
```

If you just want to know the number of lines
containing the pattern, use option "c":

```
$ grep -c 'is' text1
4
$
```

The "grep" command has some related commands, like
"egrep", for example. The "egrep" command is an
extended version of the "grep" command. It allows

92

you to do searches in the form we have seen with
the editor "ed".

The "fgrep" command allows you to search for more
than one pattern at the same time.

NOTES

Encoding of a file

9

It sometimes happens that you have a file which nobody besides you should be able to read. You will say, that is easy, just deny access to the file to everybody except yourself using the "chmod" command. Well. that is right, but it might happen that someone gets hold of your password, and he can then read your file nevertheless. Besides that, the system operator can always read your files.

To solve this problem, UNIX offers the "crypt" command which encodes a certain file.

When you use the "crypt" command to encode a file, the command will ask for a key (like a password). Once the file is encoded, the only person who can change it back to a readable format is the one who knows the keyword. When you enter the keyword, it is not displayed on the screen, just like when you enter your password when you log in.

Example:

```
$ crypt < copy > copy.crpt
Enter key:apple        ("apple" is not displayed)
$
```

What happened?
The "crypt" command got the file "copy" as its input. The output of the command (the encoded file) goes to the file "copy.crpt". The keyword is "apple".

Now let's check the encoding:

    $ cat copy.crpt

(a lot of "garbage" appears on the screen at this
point)

    $

As you can see the encoded file became completely
unreadable. The next example shows how we can decode
the encoded file:

```
$ crypt < copy.crpt
Enter key:
This text is used to show the different commands of the
UNIX standard editor.
The editor is called with "ed", usually followed by a file name.
Although this editor is a so-called line oriented editor
it is very powerful because of its many commands.
We will talk about the majority of these commands in this chapter.
You might ask yourself why it is so important to know the
editor first of all.
The answer to this is, that the editor allows you to write data,
or programs, or texts to the floppy disk or to the fixed disk.
$
```

As you can see the "crypt" command is used the same
way for decoding as it is used for encoding. The
only difference is that in decoding, the encoded
file is used as the input to the command and the
output is the decoded file.

Now we can delete the not encoded file reassured.

What happens if a wrong keyword is entered?

    $ crypt < copy.crpt
    Enter key:cuckoo   ("cuckoo" is not printed)

    (garbage is displayed again)

    $

As you can see your text has not been decoded
correctly.

96

10

Survey of the most important UNIX commands

NOTES

Name:
    at - execute command at certain time

Format:
    at time [day] [command]

Description:
Command "at" allows you to define a time at · which
you want to execute a certain command or a sequence
of commands. Process "/etc/cron" periodically checks
whether a command is to be executed and, if it is,
it arranges for the execution of the command or the
commands.

Example:

```
$ at 1200
echo "It is now noon"
<Ctrl-D>            (press the Ctrl-key and the D-key)
$
```

Around noon the message "It is now noon" will appear
on the screen. If no input files are specified, the
standard input device (keyboard) is used. <Ctrl-D>
marks the end of the input.

CAL

Name:
    cal - output of a calendar

Format:
    cal [month] year

Description:
Command "cal" generates a calendar for the year
specified. If a month is also specified, a calendar
just for this month is generated. For the year you
can enter any number from 1 through 1999; for the
month you can use 1 through 12.

Example:

```
$ cal 11 1984
     November 1984
  S  M Tu  W Th  F  S
              1  2  3
  4  5  6  7  8  9 10
 11 12 13 14 15 16 17
 18 19 20 21 22 23 24
 25 26 27 28 29 30
```

This shows a calendar for November 1984.

NOTES

CAT

Name:
    cat - displays contents of a file

Format:
    cat [file]

Description:
Command "cat" is used to display the contents of a
file. You can specify more than one file. In this
case, the contents of the different files are
displayed in the sequence of their names.

Example:

$ cat part1
The UNIX edit?r "ed"

The editor is called with "ed", usually followed by a FILE name.
This line was changed with the change command.
This text contains typos.
$

This command displays the contents of the file
"part1".

$ cat copy part1
This text is used to show the different commands of the
UNIX standard editor.
The editor is called with "ed", usually followed by a file name.
Although this editor is a so-called line oriented editor
it is very powerful because of its many commands.
We will talk about the majority of these commands in this chapter.
You might ask yourself why it is so important to know the
editor first of all.
The answer to this is, that the editor allows you to write data,
or programs, or texts to the floppy disk or to the fixed disk.
The UNIX edit?r "ed"

The editor is called with "ed", usually followed by a FILE name.
This line was changed with the change command.
This text contains typos.
$

This command displays the contents of the file
"copy" immediately followed by the contents of the
file "part1".

If you use the ">" command, the contents of the two
files are sent to the file specified:

```
$ cat copy part1 > both
$
```

The file "both" now contains the contents of both
file "copy" and file "part1".

CD

Name:
    cd - change current directory

Format:
    cd [directory]

Description:
Command "cd" changes the current directory to the
directory specified. If no directory is specified
with command "cd", the home directory is assumed.
You may check which is your home directory with the
following command:

    $ echo $HOME
    /usr/elcomp
    $

The path to the home directory is stored in the
Shell variable HOME.

Example:

    $ cd /usr/elcomp/texts
    $

The current directory has been changed by the above
command to "/usr/elcomp/texts".

NOTES

CHMOD

Name:
    chmod - change file attributes

Format:
    chmod mode file ...

Description:
This command changes the UNIX file attributes (check chapter "UNIX file system" for details).

The parameter "mode" has the following format:

    [who] op what [op what] ...

"op" stands for a "-" or a "+", it defines whether permission is given or taken away. "what" defines which right (read, write, execute r,w,x) is given to/taken away from the group of users "who". If "who" is not specified, the command is used towards the owner of the file. "who" can be "g" (group of which owner is part), or "o" (all other groups), or "a" (all users).

Command "chmod" is described in more detail in the chapter "UNIX file system".

Example:

    $ chmod a+w text1
    $

This command changes the access permissions as follows:
All users of the system now have permission to write (change) to the file "text1".

COMM

Name:
    comm - displays common lines of two files

Format:
    comm [-123] file1 file2

Description:
This command gives you three types of output:

- all lines that are only in the first file
- all lines that are only in the second file
- all lines that are in both files

The character "-" stands for standard input (keyboard). Options 1,2, and 3 allow you to suppress parts of the output. Thus, "comm -123" doesn't do anything.

Example:

The examples we have used so far are not very suitable for a demonstration of this command, because the lines are too long to be displayed three columns per line. For this reason, we will use an example which uses the "-12" option, so that only the common lines (lines that are in both files) are printed.

```
$ comm -12 copy text2
it is very powerful because of its many commands.
We will talk about the majority of these commands in this chapter.
or programs, or texts to the floppy disk or to the fixed disk.
$
```

CP

Name:
    cp — copy one or several files

Format:

    cp file1 file2

    cp file ... directory

Description:
In the first version, a copy of the first file
(file1) is created under the name "file2". In the
second version, the file or the files are copied to
the specified directory where all files keep their
old names.

Example:

    $ cp text1 copy
    $

This command creates a copy of file "text1" under
the name "copy".

If we want to do an example with the second version,
we have to create a directory first. You can try
that by yourself.

NOTES

CRYPT

Name:
    crypt - encodes a file

Format:
    crypt [key]

Description:

Command "crypt" encodes the input and sends the
output to the file specified. The keyword is not
displayed. This command is described in more detail
in an earlier chapter.

Example:

    $ crypt < text1 > text1.crypt
    Enter key:secret   ("secret" is not displayed)
    $

The file "text1.crypt" contains the encoded text
now. If you want to decode this text, the same
command (crypt) is used:

```
$ crypt < copy.crpt
Enter key:
This text is used to show the different commands of the
UNIX standard editor.
The editor is called with "ed", usually followed by a file name.
Although this editor is a so-called line oriented editor
it is very powerful because of its many commands.
We will talk about the majority of these commands in this chapter.
You might ask yourself why it is so important to know the
editor first of all.
The answer to this is, that the editor allows you to write data,
or programs, or texts to the floppy disk or to the fixed disk.
$
```

It is important that you don't forget the keyword
(in our case the word "secret"). Without this
keyword, the file can never be decoded again.

DATE

Name:
    date - displays current date and time

Format:
    date

Description:

Command "date" displays the current date and the time of day. The system operator is the only person who can change the date and the time using this command.

Example:

    $ date
    Wed Jul 25 11:50:33 1984
    $

NOTES

DF

Name:
    df - display number of free blocks on the fixed
disk

Format:
    df

Description:

Command "df" displays the number of blocks available
on the fixed disk.

Example:

    $ df
    /   (/dev/root):   4057 blocks
    $

NOTES

DU

Name:

   du - displays the number of blocks used by a file
or by a directory

Format:
   du [-s][-a][name]

Description:

Command "du" (disk usage) checks the number of
blocks used by the file or directory specified. If
no file or directory is specified, the current
directory (.) is used. Command "du" also shows us,
whether the name specified is a directory or a file.

Option "s" shows only the totals (no
subdirectories). Option "a" shows all files.

Example:

```
$ du /usr/elcomp
6         /usr/elcomp/bin
1         /usr/elcomp/public
14        /usr/elcomp/texts
30        /usr/elcomp
$
```

This example shows the directories with the numbers
of blocks used. The last line (/usr/elcomp) shows

the total, which is 30 blocks in this case.

```
$ du -a /usr/elcomp
1          /usr/elcomp/.cshrc
1          /usr/elcomp/.login
1          /usr/elcomp/.logout
1          /usr/elcomp/.profile
1          /usr/elcomp/bin/ex1
1          /usr/elcomp/bin/ex2
1          /usr/elcomp/bin/ex3
1          /usr/elcomp/bin/ex4
1          /usr/elcomp/bin/ex5
6          /usr/elcomp/bin
1          /usr/elcomp/public
1          /usr/elcomp/lsout
1          /usr/elcomp/error
0          /usr/elcomp/nohup.out
1          /usr/elcomp/texts/cat+grep
2          /usr/elcomp/texts/text1
4          /usr/elcomp/texts/text2
1          /usr/elcomp/texts/part1
1          /usr/elcomp/texts/outp
1          /usr/elcomp/texts/prlpr
1          /usr/elcomp/texts/text3
2          /usr/elcomp/texts/text1.crpt
14         /usr/elcomp/texts
1          /usr/elcomp/letter
1          /usr/elcomp/dead.letter
30         /usr/elcomp
$
```

Option "a" shows all files in all subdirectories
along with the numbers of blocks used.

ECHO

Name:
    echo - displays parameters given with the command

Format:

    echo [-n] parameter

Description:

Command "echo" displays its own parameters. Option "n" removes line feeds.

Command "echo" is mostly used in Shell programs to communicate with the user or to display error messages.

Example:

    $ echo -n "Enter a command now: "
    Enter a command now: $

This example shows how option "n" works; no line feed is sent.

    $ echo $HOME
    /usr/elcomp
    $

In this example, a line feed is sent. The pathname for the home directory is displayed.

NOTES

Name:
    ed - text editor

Format:
    ed [file]

Description:

Check chapter dealing with "ed"

Example:

Check chapter dealing with "ed".

NOTES

EXPR

Name:
   expr - evaluates it's parameters

Format:
   expr parameters

Description:
The parameters entered with "expr" are treated as
expressions. After the evaluation, the results are
sent to the standard output device. The valid
operators are shown below:

expr1|expr2   result is expr1, if this is not empty
              or "0", otherwise result is expr2

expr1&expr2   if neither expression is empty or "0",
              the result is expr1, otherwise null

expr1 rel expr2 if the two expressions are in the
              relation specified, a "1" is the
              result, otherwise a "0" is result
              "rel" can have the following oper-
              ators: <,>,=,>=,<=, and !=
              The comparison is numeric if both
              expressions are numeric (integer);
              otherwise, lexicographical compare.

expr1+expr2   addition of the two expressions

expr1-expr2   subtraction

```
expr1*expr2  multiplication

expr1/expr2  division

expr1%expr2  remainder with integer division

expr1:expr2  expr2 is a pattern (similar to grep)
             result is the number of characters
             matching with the pattern

(expr)       expressions can be concatenated
```

Example:

```
$ a=1
$ echo $a
1
$ a=`expr $a + 1`
$ echo $a
2
$
```

One is added to variable "a".

```
$ expr 'hello' : 'hel'
3
$
```

In this example, it is detected that the first three
characters of "hello" are equal to "hel".

GREP

Name:

    grep - search for lines that contain a certain
string

Format:

    grep [option] ... string [file]

Description:

Command "grep" selects the lines from a certain file
that contain a specified string. For a more detailed
description of this command, check the corresponding
chapter in this book.

Example:

Check matching chapter.

NOTES

Name:
    kill - terminate a process

Format:

kill [-signal] process number ...

Description:

This command sends a certain signal to the
process(es) specified. If no signal number is
specified, it sends signal number 15, which
terminates the process(es). Below is a list of the
different signals and their meanings:

number	name	description
1	SIGHUP	hangup signal when turning off system
2	SIGINT	interrupt signal when "Break" or "Ctrl-C" are pressed
3	SIGQUIT	quit signal when "Ctrl" is pressed system dependent, check manual
4	SIGILL	invalid instruction (machine level)
5	SIGTRAP	TRAP instruction
6	SIGIOT	IOT instruction
7	SIGEMT	EMT instruction
8	SIGFPE	error during floating point arithm.

9	SIGKILL	this stops any process, can not be ignored by any process
10	SIGBUS	error on address bus (machine level)
11	SIGSEGV	error on machine level
12	SIGSYS	error during system call
13	SIGPIPE	on a pipe it is written but not read
14	SIGALRM	signal from real time clock
15	SIGTERM	terminate signal

Signals 4 through 11 all happen at the machine level; that's why we will not discuss them in any more detail here.

Example:

```
$ sleep 30 &
123
$ kill -9 123
123 killed
$
```

The just started (background) process 123 `is terminated immediately.

LOGIN

Name:
    login - gets you into the system

Format:

login [user i.d.]

Description:

This command gets you into the UNIX system. Normally the word "login" is on your terminal at the time you want to log in so that you don't have to enter the command itself. Once you are logged in, it is possible to log in as a different user by entering the command "login" followed by the other user's i.d.

This command starts a process (mostly a Shell process), and it also defines the home directory.

Example:

    $ login elcomp
    Password:

    XENIX Version 2.5a

    $

We have logged in again and can enter commands now.

NOTES

LPR

Name:
    lpr – send files to the printer
    (lp on some systems)

Format:

    lpr [options] file

Description:

This command sends the specified file to the printer. The command differs from system to system, so please check your manual for details.

Example:

    $ lpr text1
    $

The file "text1" is printed on the printer hooked up as device "lpr".

NOTES

LS

Name:

    ls - list contents of a directory

Format:

    ls [options] file ...

Description:

Command "ls" lists the name of the files in a directory. Below is a description of the most important options available with this command:

option	description
-a	all files, including those starting with a period (.) are listed
-l	the long version of the file name (including access permission information), the date of the last change of the file, and the owner are displayed for each file
-g	in combination with the "-l" option, the group is displayed instead of the owner
-t	instead of alphabetical order, the files are listed according to the date and time of their last change
-r	reverse sequence of files listed. In combination with the "-t" option, this means the oldest file is listed first, etc.

Example:

```
$ ls -l
total 20
-rw-rw-r-- 1 elcomp          290 Oct   9 19:13 cat+grep
-rw-rw-r-- 1 elcomp          524 Nov   1 13:41 copy
-rw-rw-r-- 1 elcomp          524 Oct   9 18:53 copy.crpt
-rw-rw-r-- 1 elcomp           71 Oct  25 09:38 crpt
-rw-rw-r-- 1 elcomp          248 Oct   9 19:13 dead.letter
-rwxrwxr-x 1 elcomp           61 Oct   9 19:42 ex4
-rwxrwxr-x 1 elcomp          103 Oct   9 19:50 ex5
-rw-rw-r-- 1 elcomp          292 Oct   9 20:04 letter
-rw-rw-r-- 1 elcomp           71 Oct  11 14:32 mbox
-rw-rw-r-- 1 elcomp            0 Oct   9 18:51 nohup.out
-rw-rw-r-- 1 elcomp          252 Oct   9 19:18 outp
-rw-rw-r-- 1 elcomp          160 Nov   1 13:12 part1
-rwxrwxr-x 1 elcomp           11 Nov   1 15:50 prlpr
-rw-rw-r-- 1 elcomp          524 Nov   1 09:02 sample
-rw-rw-r-- 1 elcomp         1087 Nov   1 13:11 text2
-rw-rw-r-- 1 elcomp          180 Oct   9 20:25 text3
$
```

No directory was specified, so the current directory
is used. Option "-l" causes the long version of the
file specifications to be printed.

```
$ ls -lg
total 20
-rw-rw-r-- 1 10          290 Oct   9 19:13 cat+grep
-rw-rw-r-- 1 10          524 Nov   1 13:41 copy
-rw-rw-r-- 1 10          524 Oct   9 18:53 copy.crpt
-rw-rw-r-- 1 10           71 Oct  25 09:38 crpt
-rw-rw-r-- 1 10          248 Oct   9 19:13 dead.letter
-rwxrwxr-x 1 10           61 Oct   9 19:42 ex4
-rwxrwxr-x 1 10          103 Oct   9 19:50 ex5
-rw-rw-r-- 1 10          292 Oct   9 20:04 letter
-rw-rw-r-- 1 10           71 Oct  11 14:32 mbox
-rw-rw-r-- 1 10            0 Oct   9 18:51 nohup.out
-rw-rw-r-- 1 10          252 Oct   9 19:18 outp
-rw-rw-r-- 1 10          160 Nov   1 13:12 part1
-rwxrwxr-x 1 10           11 Nov   1 15:50 prlpr
-rw-rw-r-- 1 10          524 Nov   1 09:02 sample
-rw-rw-r-- 1 10         1087 Nov   1 13:11 text2
-rw-rw-r-- 1 10          180 Oct   9 20:25 text3
$
```

In this example, the name of the group is used
instead of the user name. In this case we belong to
group "other".

```
$ ls -ltr /usr/elcomp
total 22
-rw-rw-r--  1 elcomp           0 Oct   9 18:51 nohup.out
-rw-rw-r--  1 elcomp         524 Oct   9 18:53 copy.crpt
drwxrwxr-x  2 elcomp          32 Oct   9 19:05 public
drwxrwxr-x  2 elcomp          32 Oct   9 19:05 texts
-rw-rw-r--  1 elcomp         248 Oct   9 19:13 dead.letter
-rw-rw-r--  1 elcomp         290 Oct   9 19:13 cat+grep
-rw-rw-r--  1 elcomp         252 Oct   9 19:18 outp
-rwxrwxr-x  1 elcomp          61 Oct   9 19:42 ex4
-rwxrwxr-x  1 elcomp         103 Oct   9 19:50 ex5
-rw-rw-r--  1 elcomp         292 Oct   9 20:04 letter
-rw-rw-r--  1 elcomp         180 Oct   9 20:25 text3
-rw-rw-r--  1 elcomp          71 Oct  11 14:32 mbox
-rw-rw-r--  1 elcomp          71 Oct  25 09:38 crpt
-rw-rw-r--  1 elcomp         524 Nov   1 09:02 sample
-rw-rw-r--  1 elcomp        1087 Nov   1 13:11 text2
-rw-rw-r--  1 elcomp         160 Nov   1 13:12 part1
-rw-rw-r--  1 elcomp         524 Nov   1 13:41 copy
-rwxrwxr-x  1 elcomp          11 Nov   1 15:50 prlpr
$
```

The contents of our home directory (/usr/elcomp) are
listed. The output is sorted according to the age of
the files in reverse order (oldest file first). Had
we left the "r" out, the newest file would have been
listed first.

NOTES

MAIL

Name:

    mail - send messages to other users or empty
mailbox

Format:

    mail user

    mail [-r]

Description:

We will only describe the "r" option here; the other
options are less important, and their description
can be found in the manuals. Command "mail" was
described earlier in this book also. Option "r"
prints the oldest message first (if there is more
than one). Normally, the newest message is printed
first.

Example:

    $ mail elcomp
    Hello Elcomp !
    Greetings to Elcomp
    <Ctrl-D>
    $

This sends a message to user "elcomp". Since we
ourselves are the user "elcomp", we can now check
our mailbox:

```
$ mail
From elcomp Wed Jul 25 16:26:23 1984
Hello Elcomp !
Greetings to Elcomp

? d
$
```

We emptied our mailbox, looked at the mail, and
"threw" it away (command "d").

MAN

Name:
    man — print manual

Format:

    man [chapter] command

Description:

Every UNIX system is equipped with a manual. If you
need information about a certain command, you enter
"man" followed by the command to be explained. The
screen will display the page number of the manual
where you can find the description for this command.
You may also define the chapter where the command is
described. If the chapter is not defined, the first
chapter is used automatically. Most commands are
described in the first chapter.

Example:

```
$ man 6 backgammon
BACKGAMMON(6)       UNIX Programmer's Manual        BACKGAMMON(6)


NAME
      backgammon — the game

SYNOPSIS
       /usr/games/backgammon

DESCRIPTION
      This program does what you expect.  It will ask whether you
      need instructions.

$
```

In this example, the game command "backgammon" is described.

MESG

Name:

    mesg - allow or deny transfer of messages

Format:

mesg [n] [y]

Description:

Command "mesg" allows you to deny the transfer of messages from other users. This is helpful if you don't want to be disturbed. This command only affects command "write", it does not affect command "mail".

Example:

    $ mesg n
    $ write elcomp
    Permission denied
    $ mesg y

In the first line, we deny transfer of messages. In the second line we check whether transfer actually is impossible. As expected, the message "Permission denied" appears. Finally, in command "mesg y" the permission is given back.

NOTES

MKDIR

Name:
    mkdir - create a directory

Format:

    mkdir directory ...

Description:

Command "mkdir" creates a new directory with the name entered along with the command. If more than one name is entered, more than one directory will be created.

Example:

    $ mkdir dir1 dir2
    $

Two directories are created: one named "dir1"; the other one named "dir2".

NOTES

MV

Name:

    mv - move or rename file

Format:

    mv old new
    mv file ... directory

Description:

In the first form, file "old" is renamed to "new".
Instead of a plain name, a pathname can be used.

In the second form, the file(s) specified are moved
to the directory specified. The files keep their
original names.

Example:

    $ mv copy copy2
    $

The file named "copy" gets the name "copy2".

NOTES

NOHUP

Name:
    nohup — executes command with low priority

Format:

    nohup command [arguments] &

Description:

The command entered together with "nohup" is executed in the background. The background process is not terminated when you log out. The output of this command goes to a file name "nohup.out".

Example:

    nohup sleep 300 &
    1234
    $ Sending output to 'nohup.out'

Command "sleep 300" does nothing for 300 Seconds. The command is executed in the background (fortunately !). During those 300 Seconds we could log out. The process would continue even if we logged out.

NOTES

PASSWD

Name:
    passwd - change password

Format:

passwd

Description:

This command allows you to change your password. It
is recommended that you change your password if you
are a new user on the system because your password
may be known by other users. The password can only
be changed if you know the old password. A password
has to be at least four characters long.

Example:

    $ passwd
    Changing password for elcomp
    Old password: (enter old password)
    New password: (enter new password)
    Retype new password: (enter new password again)

As you can see, the new password has to be entered
twice. This is to prevent erroneous inputs of the
new password. If there is a difference between the
two entries, the old password will not be changed.

NOTES

PR

Name:
   pr - print file

Format:

   pr [options] ... [file] ...

Description:

This command generates a printout of the file(s)
specified. The printout is separated into pages.
Each page gets a page number and the name of the
file, and the date and time are printed as a header
on each page.

If no file is specified, the standard input device
is used.

Options:

       -n   make output "n" columns wide
       +n   start output at page "n"
       -h   use next parameter as page header
       -wn   page width is "n" (default is 132)
       -ln   page length is "n" (default is 66)
       -t   don't print header

Besides these options there are more, please check
your manual for details. During "pr" no messages are
accepted.

Example:

The file "part1" is printed:

part1   Nov 9 14:34 1984   Last mod: Nov 1 13:12 1984   Page 1

The UNIX edit?r "ed"

The editor is called with "ed", usually followed by a FILE name.
This line was changed with the change command.
This text contains typos.

Name:
    ps - process status

Format:

    ps [alx]

Description:

Command "ps" shows the status of different processes
at   a   certain time.   The chapter named   (Processes)
describes the "ps" command in more detail.

Example:

Check chapter "Processes".

NOTES

PWD

Name:
    pwd - print name of current directory

Format:

   pwd

Description:

Command "pwd" prints the pathname of the current
directory.

Example:

    $ pwd
    /usr/elcomp/texts
    $

The directory we are currently in is obviously
"/usr/elcomp/texts".

NOTES

RM

Name:
   rm - remove file

Format:

   rm [options] file ...

Description:

Command "rm" deletes one or several files.

Options:

   -f   no warnings, even if file was protected with
         "chmod" command

   -r   delete contents of a directory and directory
         itself. This command has to be used very
         carefully, it might destroy lots of work !

   -i   interactive deleting, you enter "y" for each
         file before it is removed

Example:

   $ rm -i *
   cat+grep: y
   outp: y
   prlpr:
   part1:

```
text1:
text1.crpt:
text2:
text3:
$
```

Only the first two files were deleted; the other
files remained unharmed.

RMDIR

Name:
    rmdir - remove directory

Format:

    rmdir directory ...

Description:

This command removes the directory or the
directories specified. A precondition is that the
directories are empty.

Example:

    $ rmdir dir1
    $

The directory "dir1" got removed; it was obviously
empty.

    $ rmdir /usr/elcomp
    rmdir: /usr/elcomp not empty
    $

The directory "/usr/elcomp" is not empty, and thus
cannot be removed.

NOTES

SLEEP

Name:

    sleep - wait for a certain period of time

Format:

sleep seconds

Description:

Command "sleep" waits for the number of seconds
specified and continues normally afterwards.

Example:

    $ (sleep 10 ; echo "I slept for 10 seconds")
    I slept for 10 seconds
    $

The   computer waits 10 seconds before executing   the
next   command,   which is the "echo" command in   this
example.

NOTES

SORT

Name:

    sort - sort data

Format:

    sort [options] [+pos1] [-pos2] ...

Description:

Check for detailed description in matching chapter.

Example:

Check matching chapter.

NOTES

SPLIT

Name:
    split - splits a file into smaller files

Format:

    split [-n] [file [name]]

Description:

This command splits a file into files of "n" lines
each. The default for "n" is 1000. The new files
get the specified name which is extended by the
program. The first file name is extended by "aa",
the second by "ab", etc. If no name is specified,
the name "x" is used.

Example:

    $ split -2 text1 t1
    $

After this command is executed there will be the
files "t1aa" through "t1af". Each of these files
contains two lines of the file "text1".

NOTES

TAIL

Name:

   tail - displays the last lines, characters, or
blocks of a file

Format:

   tail [options] file

Description:

The output of this command is the first or the last
lines, characters, or blocks of a file.

Options:

   -nu   output of the last n units u

   +nu   output of the first n units u

     u can be one of the following:

       l   lines
       c   characters
       b   blocks

If no unit is specified, lines are used.

Example:

```
$ tail -6l sample
it is very powerful because of its many commands.
We will talk about the majority of these commands in this chapter.
You might ask yourself why it is so important to know the
editor first of all.
The answer to this is, that the editor allows you to write data,
or programs, or texts to the floppy disk or to the fixed disk.
$
```

The last 6 lines of file "sample" are printed.

TEST

Name:
    test - check logical conditions

Format:

test expression

Description:

Command "test" does a logical test of the specified
expression. The result of this is zero if the
expression is true, and it is different from zero if
the expression is false. For more details about this
command check "The Shell" chapter.

Example:

Check matching chapter.

NOTES

TIME

Name:

    time - determines time required by a command

Format:

time command

Description:

This command delivers three time messages after the
specified command is finished. The first time is the
time from the beginning of the command to the end of
the command. The second time is the real execution
time of the command. The third time is the time used
by the system. All times are in seconds.

Example:

```
$ time df
/         (/dev/root ):      3960 blocks

real          4.0
user          0.2
sys           0.8
$
```

In this example the time required by the "df"
command is determined. It took four seconds until we
got the message about the number of free blocks on
the fixed disk. Only 0.2 seconds of user time were
used, and the system was occupied by this command
for 0.8 seconds.

TRUE, FALSE

Name:
    true - results in a zero status
    false - results in a one status

Format:

    true

    false

Description:

"true" and "false" are used in control structures to
program endless loops.

Example:

    $ while true
    > do echo "hello"
    > done
    hello
    hello
    hello
       :
       :

The command sends an endless number of "hello",
unless you stop the program with "Break" or <Ctrl-
C>.

NOTES

Name:
    tty - display terminal data

Format:

    tty

Description:

Command "tty" displays the pathname of the users
terminal.

Example:

    $ tty
    /dev/tty5
    $

We are clearly working on terminal "tty5".

NOTES

Name:
   wc – count words

Format:

wc [-lwc] [file ...]

Description:

Command "wc" (word count) counts the number of
words, lines, and characters in the specified
file(s).

Options:

   -l   only the lines are counted
   -w   only the words are counted
   -c   only the characters are counted

If none of the options is used, lines, words, and
characters are counted.

Example:

```
$ wc text1
      11        98        661 text1
$
```

This shows that file "text1" contains 11 lines, 98
words, and 661 characters.

NOTES

WHO

Name:
    who - displays names of users on the system

Format:
    who
    who am i
    who are you
    who are we

Description:

Command "who" shows who is working on the system at
a certain time. The second form of the command shows
your own person; the third form shows who the
computer is, and the fourth form is a combination of
the second and third form.

Example:

```
$ who am i
elcomp    tty5     Jul 26 07:18
$
```

This means we are user "elcomp"; we work on terminal
"tty5", and we have logged in the 26th of July at
7:18 a.m.

NOTES

WRITE

Name:

    write — send message to other user

Format:

    write user [ttyname]

Description:

Command "write" was described in the chapter named "UNIX as a post office".

The addition of the ttyname allows you to definitely address a certain user. This is only significant if the same user has logged in on different terminals.

Example:

    $ write frank tty3 < text1
    $

This command sends the contents of file "text1" to user "frank" on terminal "tty3".

11

Three useful Shell programs

In this chapter we will show you three useful Shell programs that can be typed in with the editor.

The first program inserts a new line after a certain line. The second program shows all files in a certain directory. Files in subdirectories are shown also. Subdirectories are printed indented. The third program copies a directory, including all subdirectories, to a new directory.

Before we enter the programs we have to "export" the PATH. Since we want to be able to find this each time we log in, we have to do a change in the ".profile" file.

```
$ cd
$ ed .profile
a
export PATH
.
w
80
q
$ . .profile
$ cd bin
$
```

The file ".profile" has been changed and then executed. The programs will be saved in directory "bin".

11.1 Shell program DOUBLE

This simple program should be saved under the name
"double":

```
while read a
do
    echo "$a"
    echo
done
```

As you can see, the program only consists of a
single "while" loop. The condition in this loop is
command "read".

This command reads a line from the standard input
device and assigns the input to a variable. In our
case, the name of this variable is "a". The status
of this command is always true until we reach the
end of a file.

In the loop, the line read is sent to the standard
output device with command "echo". The second "echo"
command inserts a blank line. The program is called
with "double". If the message "cannot execute"
appears, you probably forgot to do the "chmod +x
double" command, which adds the permission
"executable" to the file "double".

```
$ double
hello
hello

Good morning
Good morning
<Ctrl-D>
$
```

As you can see, the line we entered is being
displayed again, followed by a blank line. If, for
example, you want to change a file in that way

(double line spacing for corrections), enter the following:

```
SUPER> double < part1 > part1.double
SUPER> cat part1.double
The UNIX edit?r "ed"

The editor is called with "ed", usually followed by a FILE name.

This line was changed with the change command.

This text contains typos.

SUPER>
```

As you can see, blank lines have been inserted after each line.

11.2 The Shell program TREE

The following program can be saved under the name "tree". It displays the tree structure of a directory.

```
if test $# -eq 0
then a=`pwd`
else a=$1
fi
spc=$2
if test `expr "$spc" : " *"` -eq "0"
then spc=
fi
echo
echo "$spc beginning $a"
cd $a
for i in *
do
    if test -d $i
    then tree $i "$spc    "
    else echo "$spc  $i"
    fi
done
echo "$spc end of $a"
echo
```

This program is more complicated than the first one. The first IF statement checks whether the number of parameters is zero. If it is, then variable "a" gets the current directory as its value. The Shell command "pwd" prints the working directory. If a parameter was entered with that command, variable "a" gets the value of this parameter.

After the IF statement, variable "pc" gets the value of the second parameter. Next, a rather complicated procedure is used to check whether the second parameter consists of blanks. If it does, nothing happens. Otherwise, the variable is erased (spc=).

The next two lines print a blank line and the message "beginning". The value of variable "spc" (a certain number of blanks) is printed in front of the word "beginning". After "beginning", the current directory is printed. Command "cd" changes the current directory to the directory name just printed.

Variable "i" (loop variable) then takes on all file names of this directory. The IF command in the loop checks whether a name is a directory. If this is the case, program "tree" is called again. The new directory is the first parameter. The new directory also has to be printed. The second parameter remaines the same, except that it has been extended by three spaces. The subdirectories are printed indented under their father directory.

If the file is not a directory, only the name of the file is printed, at the same indentation as the directory of which the file is part (spc takes care of that).

If all files are printed that way, it indicates that the end of the directory is reached.

Command "tree" without any parameters prints the files of the current directory. If the name of

another directory is entered as a parameter, the
files of this directory will be printed. Below is a
sample:


```
      beginning /usr/elcomp
        cat+grep
        copy
        copy.crpt
        crpt
        dead.letter
        double
        ex4
        ex5
        letter
        mbox
        nohup.out
        outp
        part1
        part1.double
        prlpr

          beginning public
            *
          end of public

        sample
        text2
        text3

          beginning texts
            *
          end of texts

      end of /usr/elcomp
```


This new command shows you the technique for a so-
called recurring command; this means a command which
calls itself. To accomplish this, a new shell with
its own surroundings is started. Variables are local
in these surroundings.

It is important that the path, as defined in variable PATH, is exported, i.e., that the same path is used in all the shell surroundings.

11.3 The SHELL program CPTREE

The name of this program is "cptree". Since this program is defined as recurring, it has to be stopped by the operator.

```
if test $# -lt 2
then echo "Usage: cptree olddir newdir"
else {
    spc=$3
    if test `expr "$spc" : " *"` -eq "0"
    then spc=
    fi
    echo "$spc cptree $1 $2"
    mkdir $2
    for i in `ls $1`
    do
        if test -d "$1/$i"
        then cptree "$1/$i" "$2/$i" "    $spc"
        else {
            echo "$spc  cp $1/$i  $2/$i"
            cp "$1/$i" "$2/$i"
        }
        fi
    done
    }
fi
```


First it checks whether two parameters were entered along with the command. If this is not the case, an error message, indicating the correct format of the command, will be displayed.

The rest is similar to the preceding program, except that the third parameter is checked instead of the second. This parameter is needed for the horizontal positioning of the output. Command "cptree" comments the copying of the single files and subdirectories. The comments are also printed indented.

190

All that is done in the next line of the program. Next, command "mkdir" is used to create a new directory. The second parameter that was entered is used here.

The directory to be copied is travelled through in the "for" loop, and it is checked for directories again. As you can see, the pathname of the current directory is enlarged by the name of the file. If the file is a directory, the "cptree" command is called recurringly. The parameter of this new call is the current directory name and the new name enlarged by the name of the same subdirectory. The third parameter is the number of spaces. This number is generated out of the old number (spc) plus three more spaces.

If the file was not a directory, it is copied with command "cp". Before that, this action is commented the same way as in the preceding example.

This program uses two tricks:

1) the recurring calls make the programming much easier

2) the whole pathname is used for copying. This name is then extended by the name of the directory, and it is handed over to the recurring call of the command as a parameter.

Example:

```
$ cptree hans neu
  cptree hans   neu
    cptree hans/buch   neu/buch
      cp hans/buch/kapitel10  neu/buch/kapitel10
      cp hans/buch/kapitel11  neu/buch/kapitel11
      cp hans/buch/kapitel2  neu/buch/kapitel2
      cp hans/buch/kapitel3  neu/buch/kapitel3
      cp hans/buch/kapitel4  neu/buch/kapitel4
      cp hans/buch/kapitel5  neu/buch/kapitel5
      cp hans/buch/kapitel6  neu/buch/kapitel6
      cp hans/buch/kapitel7  neu/buch/kapitel7
      cp hans/buch/kapitel8  neu/buch/kapitel8
      cp hans/buch/kapitel9  neu/buch/kapitel9
        cptree hans/buch/texte   neu/buch/texte
        cp hans/buch/texte/beispiel  neu/buch/texte/beispiel
        cp hans/buch/texte/teil1  neu/buch/texte/teil1
        cp hans/buch/texte/text1  neu/buch/texte/text1
        cp hans/buch/texte/text1.double  neu/buch/texte/text1.double
        cp hans/buch/texte/text2  neu/buch/texte/text2
$
```

This example does not use our familiar surroundings
because this would not be very well suited to
illustrate this command. The purpose of this example
is to show you how subdirectories can be copied with
this command.

Caution!
The new directory should not be a subdirectory of
the directory to be copied. In this case the program
would never end, and you would probably get in
trouble with your system operator, because your
command would use up more and more space on the
fixed disk.

12

VENIX/86

UNIX on personal computers

In this chapter we will share some practical hints.

During development of this book we used two different personal computers.

1) A COMPAQ PLUS, 512k RAM, 10MByte fixed disk
   VENIX 86 operating system

2) An ALTOS 586 Microcomputer by ALTOS
   XENIX operating system (by Microsoft)

In the case of the COMPAQ PLUS, you get a complete UNIX system for around $5000, and this system is portable on top of that, so that you even can take it home after work. The ALTOS 586 is a higher class microcomputer and thus more expensive.

VENIX 86 on the COMPAQ PLUS

The VENIX operating system is very similar to UNIX. It represents one of the least expensive installations of a UNIX-like operating system. VENIX 86 became available in 1983. It was the first licensed UNIX operating system available for the IBM PC and its compatibles.

VENIX 86 features full multitasking/multiuser operation. It comes with word processing, data base, utilities, program development tools, and electronic mailing. It has been equipped with some UC Berkley enhancements, such as "vi", "termcap", the "C-Shell", the realtime enhancements, and the data segment usage.

VENIX 86 is available for around $800, which makes it one of the cheapest multiuser implementations of the AT&T UNIX operating system.

VENIX is available for almost any important IBM PC/XT compatible PC:

    1) IBM PC/XT - VENIX/86
    2) Eagle Turbo XL - VENIX/86
    3) COMPAQ PLUS - VENIX/86
    4) DEC Professional 350 - VENIX/PRO

No additional processor board is required to run VENIX 86. VENIX/86 is a real UNIX operating system, not a "UNIX look-alike" or a "UNIX compatible" operating system.

Full Multi-Tasking

This allows you to run several programs at the same time. There can be several programs running in the background while you are using the system for something else in the foreground. This is useful, for example, if you are printing large text files, or if you are receiving data through a modem. You may copy diskettes in the background and simultaneously compile a C-program.

Multi User Operation

Several users can use the system at the same time. There are two versions of VENIX/86: one for up to 2 users and another one for up to 8 users. The difference in price between the two versions is about $200.

194

Background processing is also possible with the multiuser mode.

Input and output (I/O) of processes can be put together in any combination. Hook up of additional terminals is very easy; it is done via the RS232 interface.

Separation of the screen (4 times)

If you are using an IBM PC XT with an IBM keyboard and you have a graphic monitor hooked up, you can separate the screen into four single screens.

This feature should not be confused with "windowing". Here you have four screens of four different users. You can switch between the four screens by a keystroke.

Example:

You have four programs running (multitasking), and you want to be able to see the operations of the four programs.

You can also log in as four different users with one user on each screen.

It is amazing how much computing power you can get in this price range today!

Flexible command interpretation

The command interpreter, also called the Shell, allows the redirection of input and output, the working out of complicated command files, and the conditional start of other programs. External devices are treated like files (as with MS-DOS). This allows you to direct the output of one file or device to the input of another file or device.

For example, the sort routine can get input from the keyboard, a file, or from an independent process. The output of the program can be used as the input for another program (piping). There can be programs (filters) in between, which filter out certain parts of the data.

PC-DOS/MS-DOS Partitions

VENIX/86 even allows you to have an MS-DOS partition on the fixed disk so that, in fact, you can have two different operating systems on the fixed disk.

What else is included in VENIX/86?

 1) four editors, including "vi"
 2) a C-compiler
 3) BASIC
 4) YACC – yet another compiler-compiler
 5) LEX, a lexical analysis generator
 6) UNIX -> UNIX communication package
 7) document formatter (nroff)
 8) Spelling checker
 9) table formatter
10) electronic mail
11) calendar and reminder
12) fixed disk – possibility of partitioning allows
    VENIX/86 and PC-DOS on the same disk
13) UC Berkeley extension including termcap, vi,
    more, and a C-Shell
14) Pipes and filters
15) PATH and I/O-redirection
16) File management including security check
    and hierarchical file structure
17) File compare, search, sort, and merge programs
18) 8087 coprocessor support

Below is a list of the commands available with VENIX/86.

Venix/86 ™

AC	login accounting
ACCESS	determine accessibility of file and directories
ADB	debugger
AR	archive and library maintainer
AS	assembler
AT	execute commands at a later time
AWK	pattern scanning and processing language
BASENAME	strip filename affixes
BASIC	*Venix* Basic interpreter
BC	arbitrary-precision arithmetic language
CAL	print calendar
CALENDAR	reminder service
CAT	concatenate and print
CB	C program beautifier
CC	C compiler
CD	change working directory
CHMOD	change mode
CHOWN	change owner or group
CMP	compare two files
COL	filter reverse line feeds
COMM	select or reject lines common to two sorted files
CP	copy
CRYPT	encode/decode
CSH	C shell command language
CU	call UNIX
DATE	print and set the date
DC	desk calculator
DD	convert and copy a file
DEROFF	remove nroff, tbl and neqn constructs
DF	disk free
DIFF	differnetial file comparator
DOS	DOS file utilities
DS	display system status information
DTREE	print the tree structure of a directory
DU	summarize disk usage
DUMP	incremental file system dump
ECHO	echo arguments

ED .... text editor
EX .... text editor
EXPR .... evaluate arguments as an expression
FCHECK .... file system consistency check and
                   interactive repair
FILE .... determine file type
FIND .... find files
FORMAT........... format a diskette
GRAPH .... draw a graph
GREP .... search a file for a pattern
JOIN .... relational database operator
KILL............... terminate a process with extreme prejudice
LD .... loader
LEX .... generator of lexical analysis programs
LINT .... a C program verifier
LN .... make a link
LOGIN .... sign on
LOOK.............. find lines in a sorted list
LORDER .... find ordering relation for an object
                   library
LP .... local printer spooler
LS .... list contents of directory
M4 .... macro processor
MAIL .... send or receive mail among users
MAKE .... maintain program groups
MESG............. permit or deny messages
MKDIR .... make a directory
MKFS.............. construct a file system
MKNOD .... build special file (device node)
MORE .... file perusal filter for crt viewing
MOUNT .... mount and dismount file system
MV .... move or rename files and directories
NCHECK........... generate names from i-numbers
NEQN .... typeset mathematics
NEWGRP .... log in to a new group
NICE .... run a command at low priority
NM .... print name list
NROFF .... text formatting
OD .... octal dump
PASSWD .... change login password
PCOPY .... copy images to/from memory
                   display
PLOT .... graphics filters
PR .... print file
PREP .... prepare text for statistical processing
PROF .... display profile data
PS .... display system status information

198

PTX . . . . permutated index
PWD . . . . working directory name
QUOT . . . . summarize file system ownership
RANLIB . . . . convert archives to random
                              libraries
RESTOR . . . . incremental file system restore
RM . . . . remove (unlink) files
SED . . . . stream editor
SH . . . . command language
SIZE . . . . size of an object file
SLEEP . . . . suspend execution for an interval
SORT . . . . sort or merge files
SPELL . . . . find spelling errors
SPLINE . . . . interpolate smooth curve
SPLIT . . . . split a file into pieces
STRIP . . . . remove symbols and relocation bits
STTY . . . . set terminal options
SU . . . . substitute user id temporarily
SUM . . . . sum and count blocks in a file
SUSPEND . . . . suspend and resume execution of a
                              process
TAIL . . . . deliver the last part of a file
TAR . . . . tape archiver
TBL . . . . format tables for nroff
TEE . . . . pipe fitting
TEST . . . . condition command
TIME . . . . time a command
TK . . . . paginator for the Tektronix 4014
TOUCH . . . . update date last modified of a file
TR . . . . translate characters
TRUE . . . . provide truth values
TSORT . . . . topological sort
TTY . . . . get terminal name
UNIQ . . . . report repeated lines in a file
UUCP . . . . UNIX to UNIX copy
UUX . . . . UNIX to UNIX command execution
VI . . . . screen oriented display editor
VSET . . . . set video mode
WAIT . . . . await completion of process
WALL . . . . write to all users
WC . . . . word count
WHO . . . . who is on the system
WRITE . . . . write to another user
YACC . . . . yet another compiler-compiler

Installation of VENIX/86

The installation procedure is described well in the accompanying manual. The installation program guides you through the installation procedure. VENIX/86 comes on 10 floppy diskettes plus one diskette with the transfer program. Once the contents of the 10 floppy disks are transferred onto the fixed disk, VENIX/86 can be booted from there. Once the system has booted, you can log in as the superuser and set up the system for other users.

How much memory (RAM) is required?

We used our VENIX/86 on a COMPAQ PLUS with 128k RAM. Although this is enough to start VENIX, it is too little for larger applications. The C-compiler, for example, does not work properly with that amount of memory.

You should have 256k of RAM or more to run VENIX/86. 512k is recommended.

Extensive set of commands

Besides the large number of commands that are standard on every UNIX system, VENIX has some additional commands from the so-called Berkeley extension. Among these commands are the full screen editor "vi", command "more", etc. Some of those additional commands can not be used on a 128k system. Besides these Berkley commands, some commands for supporting graphics have been added too. "vi" and "nroff" (full screen editor and text formatter) combined are ideal for professional word processing. Also worthy of mention is the fact that VENIX can access MS-DOS files. You can even transfer files from VENIX to MS-DOS and vice versa.

SUMMARY

One could say that it pays to purchase a VENIX system. Your system should have a memory of at least 256k; otherwise, the system will crash with larger commands and programs. The manual supplied with the system is very good and complies with the UNIX standard.

The ALTOS 586 systems

13

The 586 systems from ALTOS are systems for the serious business user. The operating system XENIX, by Microsoft (similar to UNIX), runs on these computers.

Description

The 586 family of systems consists of two desktop models. Each of those systems can handle up to five users at the same time. The built-in fixed disk has a capacity of 42 Mbyte. A second fixed disk can be hooked up, thus enlarging the capacity to 84 Mbytes.

Altos 586

All models of the 586 series have the following features:

- multi processors
  8086 as the central unit
  Z80A for I/O control
  8089 for control of fixed disk

- 512 k RAM, expandable to 1 MByte

- 5 terminals and one printer can be connected
    expandable to 9 terminals

- self test of system when turning on

- timer with battery backup

- networking possible

TeamNet II

TeamNet II by ALTOS is not one of the local area networks (LAN) with limited capabilities. TeamNet is the future-oriented network for office automation. It is a completely open and transparent system, at present installed on the ALTOS systems 186*, 586, and 986 under the XENIX operating system. Each user can access all files, programs, processors, peripherals, and other devices, as if they were all his own (a precondition, of course, is that he has access permission).

TeamNet allows a network of up to 288 users (32 computers with 9 users each) with a maximum of 32x80 Mbyte fixed disk space and 32 tape drives. TeamNet saves the user a lot of work. All information is accessible to all users. Thus, copying of files and renewed input of data are no longer neccessary. The user is always "up-to-date" anywhere in the system.

The protection schemes of XENIX are supported by TeamNet.

The implementation of TeamNet is based on the 7-level model of the International Standards Organisation (ISO Open Systems Interconnection Reference Model). On the lower levels of the implementation, a subset of the Internet Protocols by XEROX are used (Internet Datagram Protocol and Package Exchange Protocols).

Level   Description
____

7. application   application software
6. presentation   code translation, reformatting of
                        data
5. communication   virtual connections (co-operation
   control   of interaction with level 7)
4. transport   transport protocols
3. network   package transfer
2. data connection transfers information to level 1
1. physical level physical flow of information

ISO/OSI 7-level model
(International Standards Organisation Open Systems Interconnection Model)

On the application level, many networks only offer special programs for data transfer, electronic mail, or a virtual terminal, for example. TeamNet allows access to all activities in the network as well as on the computer. Existing software runs in TeamNet without problems of adaptation.

TeamNet from the users point of view

The file structure of UNIX/XENIX has been extended by a superdirectory (@). This superdirectory contains the names of all computers connected in the network (see figure below).

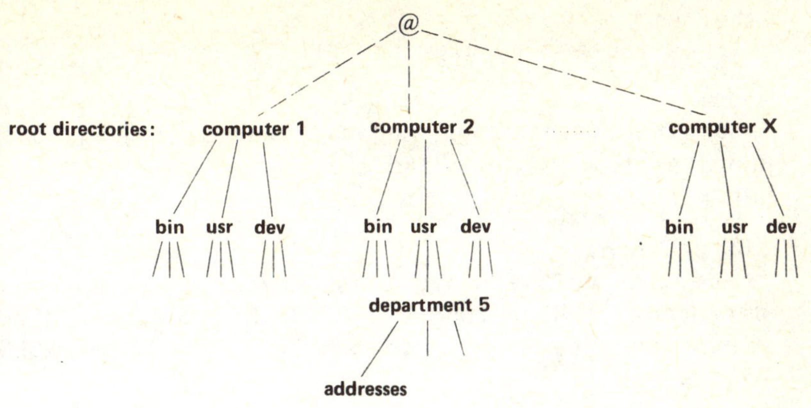

Each user has access to all files in the network through a longer pathname (via "@").

Besides the great number of XENIX commands, TeamNet supplies you with additional commands, for example one which allows you to run programs on a computer different from your own.

User friendly menus

TeamNet can be used by people with no experience with XENIX. In the "Altos Business Shell" the user is supported with extensive menus allowing him to work in the network without having to know anything about networking.

Software requirements

For the installation of TeamNet, version 2.3 of XENIX is required.

Hardware requirements

TeamNet can be run on all Altos computers of the families 186*, 586, and 986.
These systems are equipped with the neccessary hardware. The only parts that is required in addition is the TeamNet set of cables and plugs.

- Ethernet
  this is another popular network

- Modem
  data transfer through modems (1200 Baud) and the
  phone system is supported through software and
  hardware

- IBM protocol
  there is software available which generates the
  different IBM protocols (3780 bisynchron, 3270
  clustered terminal controller and SNA/SDLC
  bisynchron)

Data security

Data can be saved on the fixed disk, and the
software also fully supports saving data on tape.

XENIX

XENIX is an operating system similar to the System
V. There are two different XENIX systems available
for the ALTOS computers:

1. The runtime system containing all the common
commands, like the Shell, electronic mailing, the
editor "ed", and support for TeamNet and Ethernet.

2. The development system containing all the runtime
features, plus many additional commands and the
Berkley routines such as a complete screen oriented
editor "vi" and the Berkley termcop, which allows
you to hook up almost any terminal. Also contained
are a C-compiler and FORTRAN 77.

The two XENIX systems come with excellent manuals,
as do the ALTOS computers. The installation
procedure, in which the system has to be transferred
from floppy disks to the fixed disk, is described
clearly.